Shades *of*

JAMIE
DORNAN

Community Learning & Libraries
Cymuned Ddysgu a Llyfrgelloedd

This item should be returned or renewed by the
last date stamped below.

To renew visit:

www.newport.gov.uk/libraries

Shades *of*
JAMIE
DORNAN

JO BERRY

This edition first published in Great Britain in 2015 by
Orion an imprint of the Orion Publishing Group Ltd
Orion House, 5 Upper St Martin's Lane,
London WC2H 9EA
An Hachette UK Company

10 9 8 7 6 5 4 3 2 1

A CIP catalogue record for this book is available
from the British Library.

Hardback ISBN: 978 1 4091 5323 8

Typeset by Input Data Services Ltd, Bridgwater, Somerset

Printed and bound by CPI Group (UK) Ltd, Croydon, CR0 4YY

The Orion Publishing Group's policy is to use papers that
are natural, renewable and recyclable and made from wood
grown in sustainable forests. The logging and manufacturing
processes are expected to conform to the environmental
regulations of the country of origin.

Every effort has been made to fulfil requirements with regard to
reproducing copyright material. The author and publisher will be
glad to rectify any omissions at the earliest opportunity.

www.orionbooks.co.uk

Contents

Belfast Boy

All actors crave that one role. The role that will kickstart their career. The role that will make headlines. The role that could take them from jobbing actor to Hollywood movie star. For some, it comes at the start of their career, while for others, it can take years of auditions, bit parts and disappointments before – thanks to luck, talent, being in the right place at the right time – they get that one part they will forever be associated with; the one that launches their career into the stratosphere.

Would we know who Sean Connery was if he hadn't been James Bond? Or Harrison Ford if he hadn't played Han Solo? And would Ryan Gosling be on a million posters and desktop screensavers if he hadn't won the hearts of women everywhere as Noah in *The Notebook*? All of them had that one role that brought them to our attention, made us realise what talents they were ... and made us wonder why we hadn't noticed them before.

For Irish actor Jamie Dornan, 'that role' would be one of the most sought after of the decade: the role of Christian Grey, the wealthy entrepreneur, handsome bachelor and S&M aficionado who is at the heart of the 100-million-selling series of novels *Fifty Shades of Grey*. At the age of 32, the six-foot tall, auburn-haired actor from Belfast has moved from giving superb performances in series like *The Fall* and *New Worlds* and – slightly reluctantly, while guarding his private life fiercely – stepped into the very bright spotlight that comes with winning the role of a character millions of women have fantasised about.

The man destined to be *the* pin-up of 2015 was born, not in Hollywood, California, but in Holywood, County Down, in Northern Ireland. A town on the shore of Belfast Lough, it is situated between Belfast and Bangor, not far from Belfast City Airport and just 5 miles from Belfast itself. Baby James Dornan was born there on 1 May, 1982 to mother Lorna and father James, the first son for the couple, following two daughters, Liesa and Jessica. His grandparents, on both sides, were Methodist lay preachers, while Jamie's dad had dreams of becoming an actor before deciding to become a doctor and training as an obstetrician.

In an interview with the *Scotsman*, Jamie remembered that his dad had explored a career in acting far enough that he had auditioned, and been offered a place, at RADA after he left school. Instead, he decided to embark on a more stable career, training to be a doctor, but perhaps his brief experience of the acting world led to him being excited for his son when he chose to go in that direction.

Holywood, the town where Jamie's parents chose to raise him, sprung up around a monastery founded in the seventh century – the present Holywood Priory stands on the original monastery site. It grew into a thriving town due to its port and the introduction of a railway line to Belfast in 1848. By the

time Jamie was born, the town had become known for its mix-
ture of old and new buildings (there are some local ruins that
date back to the 13th century), boutique shops and a growing
residential area that's popular with families.

Of course, Jamie grew up with the Troubles – the conflict
in Northern Ireland that raged between Unionists and Loyal-
ists from the 1960s until the end of the 20th century – playing
out around him. Belfast saw some of the worst of the Troubles, mainly in the 1970s before Jamie was born. 'You have an
awareness of it because you know how much grief it's caused,'
he told the *Telegraph Magazine*. 'It's a tiny percentage who
have ruined it for that country, that pisses everyone else
off.'

While Jamie's dad chose to become a doctor in Belfast,
rather than pursue a career in acting, it turned out that Jamie
was born into a theatrical family nonetheless. His great-aunt
was an actress by the name of Greer Garson, a hugely popular
actress during the Second World War.

Garson's link to Ireland was through her grandfather, David Greer, who lived in Castlewellan, County Down. While
Greer – actually born Eileen Evelyn Greer Garson – was born
in London, she grew up in Castlewellan before leaving to study
at King's College, London and the University of Grenoble in
France.

She began her career in acting in the theatre, and was discovered by legendary Hollywood producer Louis B. Mayer
when he was in London looking for new talent. He signed her
to a contract with MGM in 1937, and she began work on her
first film, *Goodbye, Mr Chips*, the following year. It won her an
Oscar nomination (she lost out to Vivien Leigh for her role in

Gone With The Wind) and led to other acclaimed roles in *Pride and Prejudice, Madame Curie* and the lead role in the film she was most famous for, *Mrs Miniver*.

It was her role as the 1940s British housewife in *Mrs Miniver* that won Greer Garson the Best Actress Oscar – and got her into the *Guinness Book of World Records* for the longest ever Oscar acceptance speech. Garson's eloquent speech lasted 5 minutes and 30 seconds – and her record won't ever be broken as the Academy of Motion Picture Arts and Sciences who award the Oscars has since introduced a speech time limit (and, Jamie should probably take note for the future, if you run over the allotted speech time, the orchestra starts to play to drown you out!)

Garson was Jamie's grandmother's first cousin. While her most famous roles were in movies in the 1940s and 1950s, she continued to work well into old age, appearing in the TV series *The Virginian* in 1970, and *Little Women* in 1978, while her final role was in the show *The Love Boat* in 1982, when Greer was 78 years old. She died in 1996, but Jamie did try to contact her when he was a child, writing her a letter when she was living in Texas. 'I wrote her this letter saying I was playing Widow Twanky in our primary school production – which, may I add, I won the drama prize for,' Jamie told the *Scotsman*.

Unfortunately, Greer never got to read the letter, for as Jamie told the *Scotsman*, his family heard on the news the week before they sent the letter off that Greer Garson had died.

Jamie's dad, Jim, confirmed in a phone interview with NWP Radio in Seattle in 2014 that all the family love drama. 'Nearly all the members of the family do amateur drama – amateur drama is big in Ireland. Well, what else do you do on a wet winter's or summer's night in Ireland?'

Having shown his talent for acting at primary school, Jamie continued to study drama when he went to Methodist College in Belfast, locally known as Methody. A grammar school nestled at the foot of Malone Road in south Belfast, it's well known for the academic achievements of its students, many of whom have gone on to prestigious universities including Oxford and Cambridge. It's certainly one of the most highly regarded schools in Ireland, boasting an award-winning choir who have performed at Westminster Abbey and, more appealing for a school-age Jamie, an impressive rugby team – the school's team has won the Ulster Schools' Cup a record 35 times.

Founded in 1868 by the Methodist Church, the school was originally an all-boys institution for both day and boarding pupils, with girls only introduced later and segregated from the boys until rules changed in the 20th century. Boasting a language block, music department, indoor pool, science labs and a large gym, as well as a dedicated block for the sixth form, it's an impressive place to study, and while Jamie was there it was led by headteacher Thomas Mulryne OBE, himself a former student of the school.

Jamie isn't the only theatrically minded student to have attended Methodist College. Poets John Hewitt and Robert Greacen were students there, as were actors James Ellis (television's *Z-Cars*), Gerald Horne (best known as Mr Muscle from the television adverts), Chris Barrie of *Red Dwarf* fame, *Emmerdale* actor Paul Loughran, and Mark

Ryder (best-known for his part in *Borgia*), broadcaster Alan Green and television presenter Caron Keating.

Jamie, who was quite slim as a teen ('I was a skinny guy growing up, and I still feel like that same skinny kid now'), certainly enjoyed school and joined in the many sporting activities, including rugby and golf, which he started playing at the age of 11. Life was great, and he was popular with his fellow students – and he scored his first kiss behind the bike sheds, of course ('I was 12 or 13 years old, with a girl whose name I can't remember.')

Sadly, when he was 16, Jamie had to face something no child should have to bear – the death of his lovely mum, from pancreatic cancer. Lorna, who had been a nurse, fell ill following a weekend away in Madrid with Jamie's dad. Initially, she was diagnosed with jaundice, but soon after cancer was detected. 'It was a bizarre and huge, awful turning point in my life,' he remembered. 'The comfort was knowing that it was inoperable, knowing what the outcome was going to be rather than clinging on to some kind of hope that she was going to be with us. We had a year and a half [together].'

Jamie's dad, however, was frustrated that, as a doctor, he couldn't help his wife, as he explained in a 2004 interview with the *Belfast Telegraph*. He and his devastated family knew there was nothing that could be done, and while they all hoped for a miracle, they were all aware that realistically her diagnosis was terminal. While it was good to have hope, they knew the end was coming. 'It was important the kids had hope so that whatever time left was positive,' he remembered in the interview. 'She was amazing throughout her illness and remained a wonderful mother to the end.'

'There's no easy time to lose a parent,' Jamie has since said. 'But it's a very transitional time being that age, and a very impressionable one. It was a horrific period in my life.'

If that wasn't horrendous enough, he suffered another tragedy the following year – the death of four of his friends, who were killed in a car crash in Belfast. 'I had a terrible time when I was 16, 17,' he told the *Evening Standard* in an interview, one of very few he has given in which he talks about the awful period of his young life.

He went on to speak about having therapy to cope, not just with the sudden loss of his mother, but also the loss of his four close friends in such a shocking way. It was a lot for a teenager to deal with, especially at a time when he was facing tough decisions in his life about what to do next in terms of his future career.

Jamie also coped by losing himself in his studies, and particularly by reading books, including classics such as *Swallows and Amazons* and *The Adventures of Tom Sawyer*. A voracious reader, he still loves trying any type of book, from Ayn Rand's *The Fountainhead* to a classic like *The Picture of Dorian Gray*, one of his favourites. Once he became an established actor, Jamie went for the role of Gray in the Oliver Parker movie adaptation, *Dorian Gray*, but didn't win the part. 'I don't understand people who don't read. It's like, what else are they doing?'

His friends helped him through the tough times, too, and throughout his school years Jamie kept a close group of pals who are still with him today. 'When I go out with my mates, we're a big group of Belfast boys,' he told the *Evening Standard*. 'We can get a little, you know, hyperactive. But I tend to get my sensible head on and can be quite strict with them, like "Calm down, lads" which is why they call me "Daddy Dornan".'

He also spent a lot of his time practising his two loves: sport and drama, and decided as a teenager, with the support of his dad, that acting was what he really wanted to do. Part of the appeal, of course, was that acting didn't involve set working hours, getting up in the morning, commuting to work, and sitting at a desk all day, as he told the *Scotsman*. In fact, acting had been weighing on his mind for quite a while – not just since he had won the role of Widow Twanky in the school play – and he had become involved in local youth theatre.

Throughout his life, Jamie has had the love of his dad, Professor Jim Dornan. A colourful, caring and talkative character who is an accomplished obstetrician and gynaecologist, he encouraged Jamie to pursue his career. 'We as a family are justly very proud of Jamie – he's talented and grounded and a credit to his school (Methody), his amazing friends, his family and himself,' he told the *Irish Times*.

Clearly proud of his son, Jim said in the interview how aware he was that the death of Jamie's mother and his friends had affected his son, but had also made him a thoughtful person, one who wants to enjoy his time on earth, support his friends and family, and live life to the full.

Jamie also supported his dad when he found love again. A year after Jamie's mother, Lorna, died, Jim was giving a lecture in Dublin. An obstetrician friend of his played Cupid by suggesting a lady named Samina should attend Jim's lecture – knowing the pair would hit it off.

The pair now live in the house that Jamie's parents once

shared, in Cultra, County Down. The relationship is a very happy one, with Samina accepting that Jim will sometimes talk about his first wife, and Jim's kids – including Jamie – learning to become a family with their father's new love.

In fact, it was Samina who encouraged Jamie to follow an unexpected career – one that would indirectly lead the young Irish student to becoming Christian Grey . . .

Gigs, Girls and the 'Golden Torso'

By the time he was ready to leave school, Jamie had developed a love of rugby, acting and music. While he prepared to attend Teeside University to continue his studies (he signed up to do marketing), he spent much of his spare time with school friend David Alexander, who had been in the year below him at Methodist College. Together they formed a band – Sons of Jim (named because both of their dads' first names are, you guessed it, Jim).

'We formed the band when we were still at school, and realised we had the same taste in music,' Jamie remembered in an interview with television presenter Eamonn Holmes. 'We started to jam around and got guitars for our birthdays and had a bit of a sing song, and then it got a bit more serious.'

The pair began writing songs in their spare time, but at the age of 19, while juggling his studies and his love of sport and music, Jamie found his plans going in a completely different direction. In 2001, Britain's Channel 4 decided, in association with Princess Productions, to launch a new type of reality talent show, not to find a new pop star like *Pop Idol*, but to find a good-looking person who could start a career as a model. The series was called *Model Behaviour* and the prize for the winner would be a contract with a top modelling agency.

Jamie, encouraged by his stepmother Samina, who suggested modelling may be a way to fund an acting career, was put in touch with the show after he was spotted by a modelling agency in Belfast, and he was asked to try out by the producers of the series. He did make it onto the show but while he didn't make it to the final (he only made it through the Belfast auditions), the world of modelling opened its doors to him, and he was put in touch with renowned photographer Bruce Weber, best known for his stunning black and white photography. (His early photos of Richard Gere are often credited with turning Gere into a star.) Weber gave Jamie some modelling jobs at the start of his career, while he was still deciding what he wanted to do – go to drama school to train to be an actor, pursue a music career with his band, or become a model. By the summer of 2003, music and acting were put on hold, as he was booked on his first important advertising campaign in New York, for Asprey. He then followed this up by winning a very prestigious job – Jamie was named the new face of Calvin Klein in 2004.

The American fashion house Calvin Klein has become very famous for its sexy advertising campaigns in recent years. Founded by fashion designer Calvin Klein, the company began in 1969, selling coats and dresses, and by the mid-1970s had expanded to designing cosmetics, jeans, accessories and menswear. Klein and his company have also been credited with starting the designer jeans craze in the 1970s by putting 'Calvin Klein' on the pocket of all their jeans. One of the company's most famous early ad campaigns in 1980 featured a 15-year-old Brooke Shields modelling the jeans, with the slogan stating

'You want to know what comes between me and my Calvins? Nothing.' Made by renowned photographer Richard Avedon, the ads caused something of a stir for being so sexy and featuring such a young model. 'It was me and the jeans,' Brooke Shields remembered to *Vanity Fair*. 'We were inseparable. I didn't do a television show without that being in my bio[graphy]. I didn't go on the street without somebody saying, "Got your Calvins on?" People still come up to me and mention it.'

By the mid-1980s, the Calvin Klein label was one of the best known in the world, and acclaimed photographers such as Irving Penn, Bruce Weber, Steven Meisel and Jurgen Teller lined up to take the photos for each of Klein's eagerly anticipated advertising campaigns. One of the most famous campaigns featured then-rapper Marky Mark (now better known as actor Mark Wahlberg), as photographed by Herb Ritts, modelling Calvin Klein boxer shorts on billboards around America, and co-starring with a topless Kate Moss in the 1992 television ads that followed. Another campaign featured Olympic pole vaulter Tom Hintnaus, on the Greek island of Santorini, with a very visible bulge in his pants. When the huge billboard first appeared in Times Square it actually stopped traffic. 'I worked so hard to be the best pole vaulter in the world,' Hintnaus told the *Los Angeles Times*, 'and I ended up being more well known for putting on a pair of briefs.'

'It is simple, whoever represents Calvin becomes a star,' Sam Shahid, an art director who worked with Calvin Klein, told the *New York Times*. He was right; Wahlberg and another Klein model, Djimon Hounsou, have both since been nominated for Oscars, while Kate Moss is just one of the many supermodels who have modelled for the brand – Christy Turlington, Jerry

Hall and Lara Stone have worked for the label, too.

Being chosen as a Calvin Klein model was a major career break and seriously raised Jamie's profile. One set of photos featuring a shirtless Jamie in soaking wet Calvin Klein jeans, and a later black and white photo campaign (by photographer Steven Klein) of him in the famous Calvin Klein tight boxer shorts reclining with actress Eva Mendes garnered him a nickname: the Golden Torso.

'I think it is meant to be a compliment,' he laughed to the *Telegraph Magazine*, clearly amused by the moniker. 'I hope it is!' He also revealed that the bronzed chest he was becoming famous for wasn't all natural, and his memory of the Calvin Klein photo shoots involved being slathered in fake tan to turn his white Irish skin into a more bronzed look for the camera.

Much of Jamie's modelling didn't involve him bearing his chest, but these were the shoots that he was remembered for. 'I think I've done two shoots in my underwear ever,' he explained to the *Guardian*. 'They both happened to be for Calvin Klein. But that tag – underwear model – I just can't get rid of it.' Certainly, if you Google Jamie's name and the word 'model', you will find hundreds of photos of him in his underwear, despite his numerous fashion shoots wearing suits, jeans and, well, more clothes.

He disappointed millions of female fans in 2009 when he announced to the *Evening Standard* in an interview that he wasn't planning on taking off his shirt every time a camera was nearby. 'I've done it enough that I really don't see how it's interesting any more. People assume you're stupid enough as it is [being a male model]. Then you take your shirt off and they're like, "He must be an idiot." Seriously, people approach me and you can see it in their eyes. They're like: "Let's talk about grease and oil on your body. And aftershave. And your grooming technique".'

He wasn't kidding: during one video interview with Andrea Lavinthal, an editor for US *Cosmopolitan* magazine, when Jamie was promoting the Calvin Klein fragrance CK Free, he was asked exactly those sorts of questions, from whether he thought fragrance on a woman was important and whether he likes a woman in make-up, to what he would never leave home without (answer: his iPod, and his inhaler because he is asthmatic).

Jamie was also regularly questioned about the fitness regime that gave him the infamous torso. He revealed in an interview with *Men's Health* magazine that his favourite sports were skiing, and rugby (partly because, he told the magazine, there was a pint as a reward at the end of a match).

While rugby had been a favourite sport of Jamie's since school, he revealed it wasn't the only sport he practised to keep in shape. 'I've been into golf since I was about 11 years old and now play to a 13 handicap,' he added. 'I'll try anything once – yoga, Pilates, you name it, I'll give it a whirl and see what I can learn from it.'

He did, however, later admit that he didn't always train that hard before a shirtless photoshoot. 'Because I used to play a lot of sport I've always been in decent enough shape,' he says. 'When I used to get asked to do a bit of body work before a photo shoot, I'd lie and say, "Yeah, I'm going to the gym." I literally never did anything!'

As well as becoming known for his impressive (and often slicked with oil for the cameras) torso, one expression he used for the camera – a sort of sexy furrow of the brow – also became a Dornan trademark as his modelling career progressed. 'It's so funny. Until I do it, the photographers just aren't happy. They're like, "It's not working, it's not working." Then I look down, and then I look up, and it creates this furrow in my brow, and then they're happy!'

Whether it was his torso or his furrowed brow that appealed to advertising agencies and magazines, it didn't matter – Jamie was being booked for numerous campaigns and photoshoots and flying around the world to pose in exotic locations. In 2005 alone, he posed for Armani Exchange and *GQ* magazine, and became the face of Dior Homme's winter campaign – and still managed to fit in some time to record music with pal David for Sons of Jim.

'My lifestyle hasn't changed a cent since becoming a model,' Jamie promised Eamonn Holmes in an interview about the band. 'I'm pretty privileged, contracted to Christian Dior and Calvin Klein – I got lucky and am having a nice time of it.' While slightly uncomfortable about being in the spotlight, Jamie was clearly very aware how lucky he was and was humble about his success.

Meanwhile, David and Jamie's music career was taking off, and they were asked to support Scottish singer KT Tunstall on her tour at the beginning of 2005. 'It was brilliant fun; she's quite incredible,' he remembered to the *Scotsman* eight years later. The duo supported her on six dates and had the opportunity to see her at work on stage every night, and get to know the singer backstage as well.

They released an EP of their music a few months later, naming their label Doorstep Records after a favourite sandwich shop in Belfast, and the boys made their television debut on 7 October 2005, appearing on *The Kelly Show* in Belfast, presented by chat show host Gerry Kelly. The pair performed a song called 'Fairytale', a folk ballad with David playing guitar while they both sang. More live gigs followed, including Islington Academy in May 2006 and a performance at the Vans store in Carnaby Street in London the same month.

Modelling was still Jamie's main source of income, however, and in 2006 he was booked for campaigns with Gap, H&M, Dior Homme and the Calvin Klein campaign with a topless Kate Moss that led to rumours the pair were dating. Jamie, however, was still surprised how successful he had become as a model, as he told Guy Trebay in a *New York Times* interview in November 2006 – the interview that first gave Jamie his 'Golden Torso' nickname.

'I question why all of this has happened to me,' he said humbly, while sitting at the sleek SoHo Grand Hotel in Manhattan. 'I don't see myself as particularly good looking.' Others Trebay spoke to for the feature disagreed, with *GQ* creative director Jim Moore commenting: 'In the span of 20 years, I've seen maybe four models who have what Jamie Dornan has. He's like the male Kate Moss. His proportions are a little off. He has a slight build. He's on the small side for male models. But his torso is long, and so he looks taller, and he brings a relaxed quality to modelling. He knows what he's there for, but unlike a lot of people he's not trying to be a male model. He is not *modelling*.' Perhaps the fact that Jamie didn't see himself as a model made him a more perfect one – it wasn't his lifelong dream to pose in front of a camera in designer clothes, so he didn't feel the pressure some of his fellow models did to succeed, and was therefore more relaxed on set when the camera pointed his way.

Jamie's biggest success to date was the Dior Homme fragrance campaign, as fragrance adverts run for long periods of time, meaning the models get paid more. It was the Dior campaign therefore that allowed Jamie to buy a home in Notting Hill. In the interview with Trebay, Jamie explained that numerous models had auditioned for the job but one by one they were eliminated until people until it was down to just two possibilities – and Jamie was one of them. When, eventually, Jamie was chosen, he was surprised because, in his opinion, as he told Trebay, 'I'm not the best looking guy around.'

Jamie may not have thought he was great looking, but everyone else disagreed. By the end of 2006, he was one of the most sought after male models in the world, much to his and his family's amusement. 'I hope they [my parents] are proud,' he said of his modelling career. 'They're sort of bemused by it as much as I am. None of their friends have sons doing the same thing, so it's a funny thing for them to talk about.'

Jamie not only ended up appearing in every high-fashion magazine as a model, his name also began cropping up in the tabloids, linked to both Sienna Miller and Kate Moss, although he said in an interview with the *Evening Standard* he had only worked with Kate Moss and he never really got to know her. He seems to have been amused to see his name in the papers linked with someone he had met for one day, and Jamie certainly saw the funny side in the interview. 'My friends ring up asking why I didn't tell them I was going out with Kate Moss!' In fact, Jamie admitted he wasn't the love affair type, and wasn't very good at asking girls out on dates anyway. But it didn't stop the tabloid speculation.

Another lady he was linked with was Hollywood wild child Lindsay Lohan. While gossip websites speculated that Jamie and Lindsay were briefly a couple in 2006, it wasn't until March 2014 that it actually made headlines around the world – and all because of a piece of paper that Lindsay had written on.

Born in 1986, Lindsay Lohan had begun her career as a child model at the age of three, and had been a Hollywood star since the age of 11, when she appeared as twins in the Disney movie *The Parent Trap*. Her career went from strength to strength with movies such as the remake of *Freaky Friday*, the teen comedy *Mean Girls*, and *Herbie: Fully Loaded*, but by the time she was 20 she was already gaining a reputation for being somewhat erratic on set, and she also went into rehab for the first time.

In the years that have followed, Lindsay has been known more for her tabloid escapades and court cases than for her career. She has been arrested for driving under the influence of alcohol on more than one occasion, was sent to jail for violating the terms of her probation on another charge, and was also charged with stealing a necklace from a designer jewellery store. However, it was a note that Lindsay scribbled on a night with friends in 2013 that put her – and her supposed relationship with Jamie – back into the tabloid headlines in 2014.

The note was a list of 36 names, supposedly in Lindsay's handwriting. The names were allegedly those of her celebrity lovers, apparently idenitified for her friends during a night on the town. When the list was printed in *In Touch* magazine, some of the names were blurred for legal reasons, but the ones that were clear to read included the late Heath Ledger, actor James Franco, singer Justin Timberlake, Irish actor Colin Farrell, singer Adam Levine and . . . Jamie Dornan.

Lohan appeared to confirm the list was real on her reality show, stating: 'That was actually my fifth step in AA [Alcoholics Anonymous] at Betty Ford. And someone, when I was moving [house] during the show, must have taken a photo of it. And so that's a really personal thing and it's really unfortunate . . .' (Lohan is referring to the 12-step program practised by Alcoholics Anonymous. Step five is to admit your wrongs to God, yourself and another human being.)

While Jamie kept a dignified silence about Lindsay's list, one star on it, James Franco, commented to *Los Angeles* magazine that 'Lindsay herself has told lies about me with her people-she's-slept-with list,' leading many people to believe the whole list was possibly a publicity stunt.

With his modelling star on the rise, Jamie barely had time for a relationship anyway, and unfortunately his schedule also meant that making time for Sons of Jim was getting more and more difficult. Eventually, Jamie and David decided that the band should split up at the end of 2008, so that Jamie could continue with his modelling career and focus on what he really wanted to do – acting.

He told the *Scotsman* in 2013 that he decided to bring an end to Sons of Jim, partly because there were other people involved, including his singing partner, and he didn't have the time to commit to the band anymore.

Jamie also commented about the band in 2012, stating 'I did

have a band . . . a terrible band! I sung and played the guitar and a whiney harmonica. I would have enjoyed the band more if we'd been good. You need to believe you're the best band in the world for it to work – even if you're not. I just didn't believe in what we did.'

In an interview with *Nylon* magazine, Jamie talked about what he really wanted to do, and it wasn't modelling, partly because he didn't think it was a career for a man. 'You hear about these guys that just model, and I wonder what else they do as it takes up so little time!' he commented, adding that while modelling had been a very good career move for him, and it had been fun and interesting, it wasn't where his aspirations lay. Acting was his real ambition; although many of the roles he would have loved to have played had already been done so well, such as Marlon Brando's performance as Stanley in *A Streetcar Named Desire*.

In the meantime, his modelling portfolio was becoming even more impressive. Campaigns for Armani Jeans, Aquascutum and Armani were followed by another Calvin Klein underwear campaign in 2009, co-starring actress Eva Mendes. 'We were in Palm Springs for a whole week, the sun was shining and it was easy to get to know her,' he told Scott Wimsett from *Bespoke Banter*. 'She's very fun.'

Jamie was also asked to judge potential models – reliving his beginnings in modelling when he had auditioned for *Model Behaviour*. In the summer of 2009, Calvin Klein launched a competition to find a new male model, and Jamie, Select Model Management and Calvin Klein himself would decide who it would be. The competition was open to men from nine countries (England, France, Germany, Russia, Greece, Holland,

Italy, Spain and Sweden), and the competition was named '9 Countries, 9 Men, 1 Winner', with the winning man not only getting a year's contract with Calvin Klein, but also a trip to South Africa for him and a friend (runners-up got a year's supply of CK pants). 'I'll probably help them find someone that puts me out of a contract,' Jamie laughed at the time.

Of course, the winner Jamie helped choose, Laurence Cope from England, could only hope that he would have as successful a modelling career as the man who had picked him . . .

Getting Personal With Keira Knightley

Modelling had taken Jamie all around the world, but it was his first major job in August 2003 that changed his personal life, as well as his professional one. Photographed by renowned artist Bruce Weber for the latest ad campaign for Asprey, the British jewellers, Jamie was joined on his first professional photoshoot by the hottest actress of that year, Keira Knightley, and the two soon became a couple away from the cameras.

At the time they met, Keira was the name on everyone's lips as just weeks earlier, her latest movie, *Pirates of the Caribbean: The Curse of the Black Pearl,* had opened around the world. Just 18 when she met Jamie, who is three years her senior, she was already an old-hand at acting, having appeared in her first role at the age of just nine.

Born in Middlesex on 26 March, 1985, brunette Keira had a very different background to her new boyfriend. The daughter of Scottish playwright Sharman Macdonald, best known for plays *The Winter Guest* and *Wild Flowers,* and British TV actor Will Knightley, who has appeared in series such as *The Bill, Cracker* and *Casualty,* Keira knew she wanted to be an actress from a very early age and first asked her parents if she could have a theatrical agent at the age of three (they said no and made her wait until she was seven). 'They had agents calling the house all the time and I thought it was unfair that I didn't have one,' she told the *Boston Globe* in 2005.

After being diagnosed with dyslexia at the age of six, her mother encouraged her to continue to study and read every day and told the aspiring star that she could act during the summer holidays as reward for her hard work ('but if you drop your grades, you're not allowed to act and go up for parts,' Keira remembered). 'I was so single-minded about acting. I drove myself into the ground trying to get over dyslexia and when I finished school I had the top grades.'

While still at school, the young Keira appeared in television commercials and scored her first credited acting role at the age of eight in the *Screen One* drama *Royal Celebration*, followed by a small role in the 1995 TV movie *A Village Affair*. More roles followed, including a bit part in an episode of UK police drama series *The Bill*, a part in the mystery thriller *Innocent Lies* and the role of the Princess in the kids' family movie *The Treasure Seekers*, alongside British actors James Wilby, Gina McKee, Peter Capaldi and Felicity Jones. However, it was a small role in a 1999 film that first brought her to the attention of Hollywood.

Filming began on the eagerly anticipated *Star Wars Episode I: The Phantom Menace* in June 1997, when Keira was 12. It was a gigantic project, filming at Leavesden Studios in England, as well as Tunisia and Italy, and featuring an impressive cast that included Liam Neeson, Ewan McGregor and Samuel L. Jackson. In a pivotal role was 16-year-old Natalie Portman, playing the young Queen Amidala, who would grow up to be the mother of Luke and Leia Skywalker. *The Phantom Menace*'s producers needed another actress who looked like Natalie to play her handmaiden Sabé (with whom she swaps places) and Keira won the role.

She certainly looked like Natalie Portman – even Keira's own mother couldn't tell them apart when they were both in full Amidala make-up. 'We [Natalie and I] were both wearing the same costume,' Keira remembered in an interview, 'and we were stood next to each other. Mum nearly took her back [home] with her.'

Following on from the huge success of the movie when it was released in May 1999, Keira found the job offers came flooding in. She played the character of Rose in a 1999 mini-series adaptation of *Oliver Twist*, alongside Julie Walters, Marc Warren and Robert Lindsay; appeared in the teen horror *The Hole* when she was 16; and in 2002, aged just 17, she won her first lead role in the smash-hit movie *Bend It Like Beckham*.

Just as Jamie's modelling career was taking off around the world, so was Keira's acting career. *Bend It Like Beckham* was the story of young British Sikh girl, Jess (Parminder Nagra), who goes against the wishes of her traditional parents and plays women's football. It co-starred Keira as Jules, who becomes Jess's best friend when they bond over the love of the game – only to fall out when they both fall for their coach, Joe (Jonathan Rhys Meyers). A small-budget movie released in the spring of 2002, it became a smash hit, winning rave reviews and scoring success at the box office (it cost little over $6 million to make, and made over $70 million worldwide), while Keira won the Best British Newcomer award at the London Film Critics

Circle Awards for her performance. Suddenly, Keira Knightley was the British actress everyone was talking about.

It was her casting in a big-budget Hollywood blockbuster, however, that would launch Keira's modelling career and take her to the Asprey shoot where she and Jamie would meet. In 2002, following the success of *Bend It Like Beckham*, she auditioned for the role of Elizabeth Swann in a movie to be based on the Disneyland theme park ride *Pirates of the Caribbean*. The idea for the movie had been in development for over a decade, and following flop pirate-themed movies such as *Cutthroat Island*, no one was expecting it to be a hit. Nonetheless, producer Jerry Bruckheimer gave director Gore Verbinski a big budget (reportedly $140 million) and filming was planned to start in October 2002, using locations such as the island of St Vincent, Mexico, and studios in Los Angeles.

The plot had rascal pirate Jack Sparrow helping young blacksmith Will Turner to rescue his love, Elizabeth Swann, from the clutches of the cursed crew of the Black Pearl ship and their captain, Barbossa. After auditioning for Verbinski, Keira won the role of Elizabeth and she learned that she would be starring alongside British actor Orlando Bloom (who would later be on the same Lindsay Lohan sex-list as Jamie) as Will, Oscar-winner Geoffrey Rush as Barbossa and Johnny Depp as Jack Sparrow. 'Obviously, we were looking for a beautiful young woman, but beauty alone was not enough,' producer Jerry Bruckheimer told a press conference for the film. 'Like many of the characters in this film, Elizabeth is complex, and what you see on the surface isn't everything. It was imperative that the actress understood the many facets of her character, not just the love story between Elizabeth and Will.'

'It was a lovely experience,' Keira told Alana Lee of the BBC when the movie was released. 'We shot this for about six months in LA and the Caribbean. Johnny [Depp] is fantastic. He's a lovely bloke, very funny, very down-to-earth and a phenomenally talented actor. They're all great guys and really sweet. We just all had a laugh.'

Keira did have one complaint about the filming however – she was just about the only cast member in the pirate movie who didn't get to wield a sword. 'I didn't have a sword. Am I angry about that? Yes, very! And do they know I'm angry? Yes, they do. But I still didn't get a sword. I asked every single day, anyone I could ask, if I could have a sword but I didn't get one.'

Following the release of the movie in July 2003, Keira became hot property in Hollywood and appeared on magazine covers around the world. Magazines and newspapers described her as the latest British 'It girl', and she was offered a role in the ensemble romantic comedy *Love, Actually*, alongside a starry cast that included Hugh Grant, Alan Rickman, Emma Thompson, Bill Nighy, Colin Firth and Liam Neeson. It was during filming in London that Keira was asked to model for Asprey, and she flew to Manhattan to become the face of their new campaign. 'I am flattered to be associated with jewellers Asprey, the most distinguished British luxury house,' she said at the time of her appointment. It was there that her model management team introduced her to an up-and-coming Irish male model, and she and Jamie soon quietly began dating.

They did appear in public – including at the 2004 launch of Asprey's flagship store in New York – but in interviews Keira was very guarded about her new relationship. Once in a while she would let a comment slip in during an interview – 'Jamie's great. I'm mad about him. He keeps me sane when things get stressful and we always have fun together,' she said in 2005 – but for the most part the couple kept to themselves and avoided the public eye.

However, with Keira's star on the rise, it was increasingly hard for the pair to go out unnoticed. While giving an interview to the *Evening Standard*, Jamie said that appearing in gossip magazines and tabloid newspapers with Keira was something he was indifferent to, and it seemed he was aware that being followed by the paparazzi was something they had to live with, but being such a newsworthy couple must have been hard going for two fiercely private people.

They were also both incredibly busy. Jamie's modelling work increasingly took him away from the west London home he and Keira decided to share, while she was filming movies back to back. First there was the role of Guinevere alongside Clive Owen and Ioan Gruffudd in the historical epic *King Arthur,* for which Keira spent three months training by taking boxing, archery and horse-riding lessons before filming in Ireland. This was quickly followed by a psychological thriller called *The Jacket* that filmed in Canada and Scotland, and the action movie *Domino* that took her away from home again, this time to Nevada and California.

In fact, in an interview with *Elle* magazine, Keira showed that she was all too aware that her hard-working life affected her relationships. 'It's impossible. You try to have any kind of relationship with your family, with a man, or with a friend, and you have to be on the phone and the internet the entire time.' She did see a funnier side to living with Jamie, however, identifying what his biggest complaint about her would be.

'It would probably be, 'Don't squeeze your spots', which I'm afraid has been a big thing for me for a while. I get a load of zits and I'm always squeezing them in the bathroom mirror!'

The magazine's interviewer, Andrew Goldman, also asked Keira whether she thought she made a good girlfriend. 'I'm awful. I always have freak-outs. I don't know why anyone puts up with me. I'm mostly an emotional wreck. Anyone who has ever gone out with me would tell you that I have this awful tendency to cry when I get really angry. And I can't stop.'

In the end, the combination of their clashing work schedules and their young age meant that Keira and Jamie's relationship wasn't going to last. In the summer of 2005, Jamie's spokesman made an announcement confirming the pair had split. 'Keira and Jamie have decided to call a halt to their relationship in its current phase, but they remain completely committed to each other as friends and will continue to see each other in this capacity.'

In interviews, Keira did not speak of the split but rumours flooded the newspapers. The *Daily Mirror* reported that 'an insider' had told the paper that, 'Keira's gutted. She really thought what she and Jamie had was love but it just wasn't meant to be. They both wanted it to work but in the end it was just untenable. They were having crisis talks on an almost daily basis so the decision was reached to finally call it a day.'

It wasn't until almost a decade later, with his own acting career on the rise, that Jamie finally spoke about what it was like to have a relationship with someone so famous. 'If the person you are in a relationship with has more power in terms of occupation, they don't want you to know they feel like that,' he commented. 'They don't want to think, "Oh, he must find it really awkward because I make loads of money." So you have to try to keep that to yourself and still be the man in the whole thing, which I didn't do very well.'

In an interview with the *Evening Standard*, he talked about what it had been like dating Keira and the pressure of being photographed wherever they went, which must have added strain to their relationship.

'It was a strange environment to find yourself in, being hounded and followed,' he remembered. 'It's really hideous. F**king hell, [the paparazzi] are cretins. I couldn't have less respect for those guys. There are so many ways to make a living that don't involve hiding in bushes opposite houses of 18-year-old girls with a camera in your hand. That's not making a living, that's making a choice to be a perverted f**khead.'

While the pair had gone their separate ways, and Jamie discovered that the paparazzi were moving on to their next target, he and Keira did stay in touch as their careers went in different directions. Following their split, Keira won rave reviews and an Oscar nomination for Best Actress for her performance in *Pride and Prejudice* (though Reece Witherspoon won the award for her performance in *Walk The Line*). During filming she also met the next man in her life, co-star Rupert Friend.

They were together for five years, during which time Keira's star continued to rise, with roles in two blockbuster *Pirates of the Caribbean* sequels, the acclaimed period dramas *Atonement* and *The Duchess*, and contemporary dramas *London Boulevard*, *Last Night* and *Never Let Me Go* all adding to her impressive CV. Her relationship with Rupert ended in 2010, and she went on to date Klaxons musician James Righton in 2011. The pair were married in France in May 2013.

Jamie, meanwhile, was about to get the break he was look-ing for, the break that would take him from the world of modelling to a new life working as an actor. In an interview with the *Evening Standard*, he had talked about Keira's career and commented, 'I don't think I'm ever going to be as famous as her.' Little did he know that in a few short years, it wouldn't be Keira's name on everyone's lips . . . it would be his . . .

Making *Marie Antoinette*

I n late 2005, Jamie was determined to make the transition from model to actor, and had hired an agent to help him realise his dream. At the same time, across the Atlantic in New York, a 34-year-old director named Sofia Coppola was working on the outline for a movie that would mark Jamie's acting debut.

The youngest child of director Francis Ford Coppola, Sofia had grown up as part of a filmmaking dynasty. Her cousin is Academy Award winning actor Nicolas Cage, her aunt is *Rocky* actress Talia Shire, her grandfather was the film composer Carmine Coppola, while another cousin is actor Jason Schwartzman.

Sofia's father, Francis, is probably the most famous member of the family. A screenwriter and director, he is best known for his 1972 movie *The Godfather* and its two sequels, as well as the war drama *Apocalypse Now* and teen movie *The Outsiders*. In fact, Sofia made her own movie debut as a baby in *The Godfather* during a baptism scene, and later in small roles in her father's movies *The Outsiders*, *Rumblefish* and *The Cotton Club*. In 1990, when her father was filming *The Godfather Part III*, he asked Sofia to step in when Winona Ryder withdrew from the important role of Mary Corleone (daughter of Al Pacino and Diane Keaton's characters, Michael and Kay Corleone).

It was a decision that would make headlines. When the movie was released, it received very mixed reviews, and Sofia was singled out for criticism. Janet Maslin of the *New York Times* wrote that she gave a 'flat, uneasy performance . . . Ms Coppola's uncertain presence does little but call attention to strenuous compensatory acting on the part of her costars . . .' while renowned critic Gene Siskel said she was 'out of her acting league . . . she's supposed to be Andy Garcia's love interest but no sparks fly. He's more like her babysitter.'

With reviews like that, it's not surprising that Sofia decided acting was not for her. Years later, she talked to *Guardian* journalist Ryan Gilbey about how she felt about the role. 'I didn't really think about the public aspect of it. That took me by surprise. The whole reaction. People felt very attached to the *Godfather* films. I grew up with them being no big deal.' She added, 'It makes sense that people would have an opinion about it but I got a lot of attention I wasn't expecting.'

Aside from a small role in *Star Wars Episode I: The Phantom Menace* nine years later – playing a handmaiden alongside Jamie's future ex, Keira Knightley in a 'it's a small world' sort of coincidence – Sofia retired from acting, but given her family background, it was no surprise to learn that she wanted to continue working in film in a different capacity, as a director like her father.

After making the short film *Lick The Star* in 1998 when she was 27, Sofia made her feature film debut with the critically acclaimed drama *The Virgin Suicides* a year later. It was her next movie as a director (and writer) that truly stunned, however – the 2003 drama *Lost in Translation* with Bill Murray and Scarlett Johansson. The film, about an ageing American actor in Tokyo befriending a newlywed staying in the city with her husband, was nominated for an Oscar for Best Picture and Best Director, and was awarded Best Original Screenplay.

When it was announced that Sofia's next movie as both writer and director would be a biopic of infamous French queen Marie Antoinette, there was much excitement among actors and actresses wanting a role in her latest movie. It was soon announced that Kirsten Dunst, who had starred in Sofia's movie *The Virgin Suicides,* would star as Marie, while Jason Schwartzman would play her husband, Louis XVI, and a certain newcomer by the name of Jamie Dornan had won the pivotal role of Count Axel Fersen.

With a reported budget of $40 million, this would be a grand retelling of Marie Antoinette's story, loosely based on author Antonia Fraser's 2002 biography that had a sympathetic view of the queen, who was born into the royal family of Austria in 1755.

Aged just 15, Marie was betrothed to Louis-Auguste, the Dauphin of France, who was just 14 years old himself and next in line for the French throne. The pair were actually married before they had even met! In a ceremony in Vienna Marie's brother Ferdinand stood in for the absent bridegroom in a marriage by proxy, and they were not formally introduced until a few weeks later. A ceremonial wedding was then performed on 16 May 1770 at the Palace of Versailles.

To begin with, Marie Antoinette was popular with the people of France, who were charmed by her personality and beauty, but she was less popular at court, where her lack of education counted against her, and rumours of a lack of sex life between Marie and her husband were rampant (he apparently preferred to go hunting). To amuse herself while the Dauphin paid little interest in her, Marie spent money on clothes and gambling, further incensing the court, and surrounded herself with ladies to keep her amused (fuelling rumours of lesbianism).

In May 1774, the King, Louis XV, died of smallpox and a month later, Marie's husband was crowned Louis XVI of France, with Marie becoming queen. Four years later, after many rumours that their marriage still hadn't been consummated, the royal couple announced that Marie was pregnant with her first child, a girl named Marie-Therese Charlotte, who was born in December 1778. A son, the Dauphin, was born three years later.

It was around this time that Count Axel von Fersen came to Versailles. He was a frequent visitor over the following years – so much so, that when Marie gave birth to a second son, Louis Charles, in 1785, many believed Fersen to be the father.

Of course, Marie Antoinette is most famous for how her life ended. She had fallen out of favour with the French people, who disapproved of her seemingly lavish lifestyle at a time when they were suffering due to rising bread prices following a disastrous winter, and there were financial problems nationwide caused by too many expensive wars being fought. Riots began against the crown, and by the summer of 1789 France was in the midst of a revolution. The royal family were forced to leave Versailles by a Parisian mob, and were installed in the Tuileries Palace in Paris under surveillance. One attempt to escape Paris was masterminded by her rumoured lover Fersen, but the plan ultimately failed.

Things became even worse for the royal family, and they were imprisoned in the tower of the Temple in the Marais district of Paris in August 1792. On 21 September 1792, the monarchy had officially fallen and the king was put on trial. He was executed on 21 January 1793, while Marie's trial took place in the October. She was accused of throwing orgies at Versailles, sending treasury money to her home country of Austria, incest with her son and various plots against the people. She was found guilty of treason on 16 October, and later that day she was beheaded, aged just 37.

Surprisingly, for such a fascinating woman, the story of Marie Antoinette's life had rarely been captured fully on screen. W.S. Van Dyke cast Norma Shearer as Marie, and Tyrone Power as Fersen in his 1938 biopic, and there was a French drama with Michele Morgan and Richard Todd playing the roles in 1956. One of the only other dramas to feature Marie was the two part film, *La Révolution Française*, featuring Jane Seymour as Marie, that was made in 1989, while the most recent movie before Sofia Coppola's was the 2001 period drama *The Affair of the Necklace*, with Joely Richardson as the Queen caught up in a plot by Louis XV's mistress Jeanne de Saint-Rémy de Valois (Hilary Swank).

'There hadn't been a film really about Marie Antoinette since the late thirties and it's such a visually interesting world I think to create in a film,' Sofia told an LA press conference when she was working on the movie. 'I like to see a movie where you get lost in another world and 18th-century France, with the wigs and the costumes, is so different than our daily life, I thought

it would be interesting to show that. So just when I was reading the [Antonia Fraser biography] book, I thought about it as
a film. And also for me it was a challenge personally. How do I
make a period film that isn't in the genre of period films but in
my own style? That was a challenge for me.'

Sofia had chosen actress Kirsten Dunst as her Marie, whom
Jamie would have to act a love scene with, and it was a good
choice as Sofia had already worked with her on the movie *The
Virgin Suicides*. The actress, who is the same age as Jamie,
was born in New Jersey to a German father and Swedish/
German mother. When her parents separated when she was
11, she moved with her mother and brother Christian to Los
Angeles, but she had actually begun an acting career before
she even arrived in Hollywood. In fact, while Jamie didn't
come to the world of acting until he was 24, Kirsten was an
old hand by the time she was ten. She had modelled from the
age of three, and at the age of six had made her film debut in
Woody Allen's contribution to the anthology movie *New York
Stories*. She followed this with a role as Tom Hanks' daughter
in *Bonfire of the Vanities*, and scored her breakthrough role,
aged just ten, in *Interview with the Vampire*.

That role as the child vampire Claudia, who becomes a sur-
rogate daughter to vampires Lestat (Tom Cruise) and Louis
(Brad Pitt) won her rave reviews, and also gave her a first
movie kiss, with Brad Pitt. 'Kissing Brad was so uncomfortable for me,' she said in an interview with *Interview Magazine*.
'I remember saying in interviews that I thought it was gross,
that Brad had cooties. I mean, I was ten!' Difficulties aside, the
performance won her an MTV Movie Award for Best Breakthrough Performance, and a Golden Globe nomination.

In the years that followed, Kirsten Dunst gave numerous acclaimed performances in movies as diverse as *Little Women* (with Winona Ryder and Claire Danes), the television series *ER* (as a child prostitute looked after by George Clooney's Dr Doug Ross) and, of course, as one of the mysterious Lisbon sisters in *The Virgin Suicides.* By the time she was 20, she had also starred in a major blockbuster – as Mary Jane to Tobey Maguire's Peter Parker in *Spider-Man* – and the acclaimed cult drama *Eternal Sunshine of the Spotless Mind. Marie Antoinette* would be the first time she had truly carried a movie by herself – and it required the young actress to be in almost every scene.

When Sofia was planning the shoot for the movie, she was given permission to film on location at Versailles, the stunning royal chateau outside Paris that Marie and Louis called home. In a behind-the-scenes interview on the set of the movie, Sofia explained that she described her approach for the film to the director of Versailles, and received a positive reaction to her plans and her script, possibly because no film before had really explored the history so fully from Marie's point of view. Rumour has it that the director was a huge fan of *Lost in Translation*, which is why he gave permission to allow filming at one of France's most famous tourist attractions that had also been used in movies such as *Dangerous Liaisons* and *Jefferson in Paris*.

'I feel like being in the real Versailles affected everyone working on it, and the actors,' Sofia said, clearly awed by the surroundings of the palace. 'I just think there's more authenticity than if we built it. Even the fact that you were seeing the real gardens outside the windows I think feels less artificial than if you built everything.'

Sofia Coppola's third movie would mix her own vision with the style of the age. 'Everything we did is based on research about the period, but it's all seen in a contemporary way,' she commented. 'I didn't want to make a dry, historical period movie with the distant, cold tableau of shots. It was very important to me to tell the story in my own way. In the same way as I wanted *Lost in Translation* to feel like you had just spent a couple of hours in Tokyo, I wanted this film to let the audience feel what it might be like to be in Versailles during that time and to really get lost in that world.'

Sofia wanted to try to depict the real Marie – a naïve teenager when she came to court who was trapped in a passionless marriage and who found solace in the people around her, especially Axel von Fersen. She cast Jason Schwartzman in the part of Louis, Marie's husband, and he enjoyed the role. 'I liked the idea of giving these historical figures some mouth to mouth resuscitation and helping to bring Louis XVI fully to life,' he said. 'It's not just like watching people up on a pedestal from far away – you're right in there with Marie Antoinette and Louis in their daily lives. So it's a very intimate story about something huge.'

The movie didn't follow the whole of Marie's life, instead beginning with her arrival at French court and ending when the family have to abandon Versailles. And it wasn't a typical historical movie in terms of style, either – Sofia Coppola gave the film a unique look, mixing the classical with the modern and backing it with a pop soundtrack. Elaborate wigs, intricate costumes and even shoes by Manolo Blahnik were featured in the film, with Kirsten Dunst often weighed down by both her hairpiece ('I would get sore throats every morning just from inhaling all the hairspray and stuff!') and her dress.

While pre-planning on the movie was gearing up, Jamie was rehearsing Sons of Jim songs back in London with David Alexander, and got the call from his agent that there was a part in Sofia Coppola's new movie that may be suitable for him. His was the last role to be cast, after numerous actors had reportedly auditioned for the role of Axel von Fersen but none had been chosen. Jamie was asked to fly to Paris to read for Coppola, and the next day he learned he had been chosen for the part.

First time actor Jamie had to be quickly fitted for detailed period costumes as von Fersen. Sofia imagined the character to look something like Adam Ant, with a brocade waistcoat, black frock coat and stylish hat. He certainly cast a dashing figure on set in a scene where he and Kirsten Dunst exchange glances at an outdoor party, flirting without saying a word, and later sharing a conversation that causes the courtiers to gossip and one of the ladies in waiting to defend the pair – 'He amuses her, and she likes to be amused ...' However, it is a later scene that most fans remember – and not because of Jamie's elaborate costumes. Using Adam and the Ants' song 'Kings of the Wild Frontier' as a backdrop, we see Fersen and Marie in the royal bedchamber together, secretly romancing in a field and then in bed together – with Jamie naked from the waist up.

While Jamie's role was small, that scene certainly got him noticed, and he came ninth on *Cosmopolitan* magazine's list of 30 Hottest Men due to the performance, and possibly the semi-nude scene. The film itself premiered in Cannes Film

Festival in May 2006, where it had a mixed reception, with reports that some of the (mainly French) audience booed during the movie, put off by Coppola's stylised view of a piece of French history, backed by a contemporary punk soundtrack. The French especially took a dislike to Sofia's interpretation of historical facts, with historian Jean Tulard in *Le Figaro* writing that it was 'Versailles in Hollywood sauce' while Alex Masson of *Score* wrote it had a script 'that often forgets its attempts to overthrow social order in order to become a special issue of *Vogue* devoted to scenes of Versailles.'

Sofia took the criticism in her stride and said to *USA Today*, 'I didn't know about the boos – it's news to me. But it's better than a mediocre response.' Cannes Film Festival audiences are renowned for making their opinions heard – other movies that have been booed there include *Taxi Driver*, *Pulp Fiction* (which one critic said was greeted with 'a tidal wave of jeers' when it won the Palme D'Or award there), David Lynch's *Twin Peaks: Fire Walk With Me* and Antonioni's now acclaimed *L'Avventura* – so *Marie Antoinette* wasn't in bad company.

Certainly the reception elsewhere in the world was better. Jamie and the rest of the cast attended the New York Film Festival in October 2006, where the film was shown shortly before it was released in the US to reviews that included four stars from revered critic Roger Ebert and praise from *Rolling Stone*'s Peter Travers that included: 'With lyrical intelligence and scrappy wit, Coppola creates a luscious world to get lost in.' Meanwhile, the *Village Voice* added that it was a 'graceful, charming, and sometimes witty confection,' but hinted that it would divide opinion, asking whether it was 'drop-dead hip or cluelessly clueless.'

At the box office, the movie didn't do badly, making over $5 million in its first week in the US and ultimately over $61 million in total worldwide. Jamie's first movie also won a few nominations for its distinctive look, including BAFTAs for Best Art Direction, Costume Design and Best Make-Up and Hair, and it won the Academy Award for Milena Canonero's distinctive costume design.

In the years since the movie's release, it has gone from being a film that divided critics to something of a cult phenomenon thanks to its quirky script and sumptuous costumes. It was certainly an eye-opening introduction to the world of movies for Jamie, and despite his small role, one that would lead to more acting roles in the future and – while he continued to juggle his modelling career with acting – some of his most memorable photo shoots, too.

Leading Roles

For some actors, fame can come overnight. One performance can thrust them into the spotlight, and then the phone never stops ringing as offers of new and exciting roles come one after the other. Jamie had already seen it happen to his ex, Keira Knightley, as her roles in *Bend It Like Beckham* and *Pirates of the Caribbean* had propelled her to the top of Hollywood's A-list, but like most working actors he soon discovered that it is only a lucky few who have such instant success. For every other actor, and every waiter in LA dreaming of becoming an actor, life is a seemingly endless round of auditions, getting excited about roles, discovering the director has chosen someone else, and then more fruitless auditions.

Working as a model provided Jamie with the income and work he needed to fund numerous auditions after he had finished filming *Marie Antoinette*. As he told Benji Wilson of the *Guardian* in 2014: 'Although it looks like I've only been acting a few years, we're talking hundreds and hundreds of failed auditions. I look back on it now and I don't know how anyone gets through the rejection.'

In the interview, Jamie admitted he realised how lucky he was to be able to go for numerous auditions and meetings because he was earning money as a model – many other actors, of course, have to struggle to make ends meet while trying to win a TV or movie role that will pay the bills.

In between his photo shoots, Jamie auditioned for numerous roles in both film and TV but told *Interview Magazine* that, in his opinion, he never got very good at auditioning. Some actors love that part of the process, trying out a new role and making it their own as a sort of on-the-spot test, but Jamie noted that he didn't feel he was that skilled at it, and that even after he appeared in *Marie Antoinette* and therefore had some work to show people, it was still quite a while before another acting job came his way.

In fact, it was almost two years after he had been praised for his performance in *Marie Antoinette* that Jamie was finally offered another acting role – in an interesting project called *Beyond the Rave*.

A 20-episode horror serial, *Beyond the Rave* was unusual for two reasons. It was originally made for internet broadcast, debuting on MySpace, and was produced by the legendary British film company Hammer Film Productions.

Horror fans will recognise the name Hammer as it was synonymous with gothic horror and science fiction from the fifties until the seventies. Beginning in a small, three-room office in London's Regent Street in 1934, Hammer Productions made a series of cheap, quickly made movies in the forties, before moving operations to a mansion named Down Place near Windsor that was later renamed Bray Studios. It was there that the company started to concentrate its efforts on making horror movies, beginning with a film adaptation of the BBC TV series *The Quatermass Experiment*, and continuing with *The Curse of Frankenstein*, starring Peter Cushing as Baron Victor Frankenstein and Christopher Lee as his monster. The pair would star together again in 1958's *Dracula*, and 1959's *The Mummy*, which proved big hits at the cinema with their mix of thrills, chills, horror and buckets of blood.

Over the next two decades, Hammer Productions became famous for their numerous horror movies made for small budgets, including an impressive six *Frankenstein* sequels, eight *Dracula* movies and cult classics like *The Curse of the Werewolf* (which marked Oliver Reed's first starring role), *The Vampire Lovers* with Polish actress Ingrid Pitt, and *The Two Faces of Dr Jekyll*.

By the late seventies, however, the cheap and cheerful gore of Hammer horrors had gone out of fashion as mainstream cinema competed with their own horror movies made with bigger budgets and better scripts. Hammer diversified into television with the series *Hammer House of Horror* that was broadcast in the UK in 1980 (the most famous episode being 'The House that Bled to Death', which included a scene rated as one of the scariest ever shown on British television) and featured well-known British actors in the one-hour horror episodes, such as Brian Cox, Denholm Elliott, Diana Dors, and future James Bond actor Pierce Brosnan in an early role. These episodes were followed by the feature-length TV movies shown in the US and UK as *Hammer House of Mystery and Suspense* in 1984, which ended up being Hammer's final productions in the twentieth century.

It wasn't until more than two decades later that Hammer announced they were in the production business once more.

Their first project would be *Beyond the Rave*, a vampire story told in episode form (20 instalments, each one about four minutes long) that would premiere online via MySpace in April 2008.

Written by Tom Grass and Jon Wright, *Beyond the Rave* tells the story of soldier Ed, as played by Jamie, who is flying out to Iraq in the morning. Before he goes, he's looking for one final night of fun, but first he has to track down his girlfriend Jen (Nora-Jane Noone), who has been partying with a group of ravers led by a mysterious man named Melech (Sebastian Knapp) in a remote forest. However, her companions are not quite what they seem – they are vampires who lure crowds to their raves, ready to feast on them. It's down to Ed and his friend Necro (Matthew Forrest) to save Jen, and themselves, from the deadly fanged creatures.

'The original idea for the movie came to me when I was locked in a car, at a rave in Wiltshire, and everyone outside was really scary,' remembers writer Tom Grass. 'That was the genesis, originally with scarecrow zombies, and then we decided on vampires.'

Once the script was written, the director and producers set about finding their cast and settled on Jamie for the lead role of Ed. 'I met the producer at my sister's wedding and was very fond of him,' Jamie remembers. 'I liked what he was trying to do with the project, and after plenty of drink, I said I'd be involved. Then I was involved and it was a mad shoot! The whole shoot was a night shoot. I was sleeping all day, having no life, and then getting up, going to work at six in the evening and coming home at six in the morning – very strange. I don't remember a great deal about that time,' he laughed. 'But I made good friends. We were brought together through the lack of sleep.'

'I encouraged all the actors to change the characters and modify them and make them their own and bring them to life. They took the script to the next level,' said director Matthias Hoene about his cast, which also included *24*'s Tamer Hassan and *The Descent*'s Nora-Jane Noone. The shoot mainly took place in Black Park, in Buckinghamshire in September 2007, with one of the early scenes featuring Jamie, in a dream sequence, firing a machine gun at one of the vampires. 'For anyone who has never fired a gun before, it's fun,' said Jamie on the set. 'Still, don't think I want to do one in real life, though.'

Jamie's character, Ed, is the most normal character in a film populated with vampires – he's just a regular guy who is in love with a girlfriend who has truly got friendly with the wrong crowd. While it was nice for Jamie to have the lead role, he did admit that he would have preferred his character to have had a racier plotline, and perhaps get turned into a vampire: 'I wanted some of those teeth!'

The rave itself was filmed in a building in Plumstead, East London, with hundreds of extras and music chosen by renowned DJ Pete Tong. Much of the shoot, of course, took place at night. This meant all the cast had to adapt to filming at night and sleeping during the day, much like the vampire characters many of them played.

In an interview with the *Daily Telegraph*, Jamie talked about the contrast of working on a horror movie for Hammer after appearing in costume drama *Marie Antoinette*. 'I had just come out of a nice family period drama, and that was partly why I wanted to do something like *Beyond the Rave*. I was also intrigued by the whole webisode thing. The shoot felt a lot faster than anything I'd done before. There was a real buzz on set because everything was so speedy. But then, if you're going to make an impression in a five-minute episode, it's got to be pretty sharp. It was new territory for everyone.'

Of course, being a Hammer production about vampires meant that there was blood and gore as people are attacked, swords are waved, and heads chopped off. 'It was quite hard to take it seriously when you're being attacked by a mad vampire wielding two samurai swords,' Jamie laughed.

Director Matthias Hoene told the *Telegraph* that delivering a series of short episodes for MySpace was very different from making a conventional movie, because you have to grab the viewer's attention straight away. Normally, whether it's a TV episode or a movie, directors have the time to spend setting up the characters and the background to a story, but in a five-minute webisode you have to cram in character development, fun and action in a very short space of time to hook the viewer in so they will want to watch the next episode.

Throughout the 20 episodes Jamie's character Ed has to find his girlfriend, who has gone off to the rave in the middle of a forest, win her back from the charms of Melech (whom she doesn't know is a vampire), and then battle lots of grue-some vampires. It turned out that it wasn't the fight scenes – or a chase on a quad bike – that Jamie enjoyed shooting the most, but the rave scenes which were so realistic that the cast danced about, watched the light show and all forgot they were filming.

As a fan of folk music, Jamie admitted he had only just got

into dance music in his mid-twenties, shortly before filming began. 'Now I go to Fabric, and Ibiza, and it's fun. It's a fun thing to be part of and I now think, why did I waste 24 years of my life not being into this?'

Jamie clearly enjoyed the role, and joked on the red carpet when the series was released about who he would bite ('Angelina Jolie, she looks like she's got quite a nice neck for that kind of action') and who he would stake ('I have a real problem with Usher! It's terrible, I have never met the guy, he might be nice, but his whole kind of "thing" I don't really get. Terrible, terrible. I'm sorry, Usher!')

While the movie wasn't a huge smash hit when it was released in April 2008, it did win some positive reviews and a cult following online. The Horror Asylum website called it a 'triumphant return' for Hammer Films and James Gracey of horror website Behind The Couch wrote that it had 'its fair share of effective moments'. Noted horror-film critic Kim Newman, meanwhile, gave the movie a mixed review, and commented that 'Dornan's potentially interesting hero suffers because the film can't slow down to let his neuroses register.'

Jamie had little time to worry about the reviews, however, as he was already working on his next movie. Leaving the woods of Buckinghamshire for the coastal beauty of Norfolk, he was off to work on a rather different film to a Hammer horror, a small-scale drama called *Shadows in the Sun*.

Set in the sixties on the East Anglian coast during one idyllic summer, the movie tells the story of elderly Hannah, who lives a peaceful and happy life in the rambling home she once shared with her late husband. She's helped by her friend, the much younger and carefree drifter Joe, but when Hannah's grown son Robert arrives with his two children for the summer, he is not pleased by Hannah and Joe's close friendship, nor how friendly his young son and teenage daughter become with this stranger in his mother's life.

The movie teamed Jamie, as drifter Joe, with *Howards End* actor James Wilby (as Robert) and actress Jean Simmons as Hannah, in what was to be her final role. While Jamie had acted alongside well-known current Hollywood actors in *Marie Antoinette*, he now had the chance to appear with a true screen legend who began her career when she was just 15.

Born in North London in 1929, Jean Simmons was the youngest of four children. She began her acting career after director Val Guest spotted her in class at the Aida Foster School of Dance, and cast her in the 1944 movie *Give us the Moon*. After a number of small roles, in 1946 Jean won the part of the young Estella in director David Lean's acclaimed *Great Expectations*, and followed it a year later with Michael Powell and Emeric Pressburger's *Black Narcissus*. The story of a group of Anglican nuns (including one acted by Deborah Kerr) who set up a school and hospital in a remote part of the Himalayas, it co-starred Jean in the role of Kanchi, a local dancing girl. Filmed in Pinewood Studios rather than some exotic location, Jean remembered her first day on set: 'I came on set and saw these plastic mounds and wondered what the hell it was. Then the cinematographer said, 'Come and look through the camera.' I looked and it was the Himalayas – quite extraordinary!' Numerous memorable performances followed, including Ophelia in Laurence Olivier's 1948 *Hamlet* (for which she received an Oscar nomination), the lead in the original *The Blue Lagoon*, and a starring role alongside Stewart Granger in the 1949 romance *Adam and Evelyne*.

Jean had met British actor Stewart Granger four years before when they had worked on *Caesar and Cleopatra* together, and in 1950 they were married (they divorced in 1960). They made two more films together, and Jean also starred with some of the biggest names in Hollywood during her twenties and thirties – Robert Mitchum (*Angel Face*), Spencer Tracy (*The Actress*), Richard Burton (*The Robe*), Frank Sinatra and Marlon Brando (*Guys and Dolls*), Burt Lancaster (*Elmer Gantry*), Cary Grant (*The Grass is Greener*) and Gregory Peck (*The Big Country*).

It was a film Jean made in 1960 that remains one of her best-loved films, however. She starred as Varinia, the love of slave Spartacus in the movie of the same name. With a cast that included Kirk Douglas, Laurence Olivier, Peter Ustinov and Tony Curtis, it was a huge box-office hit and remains a classic to this day, with the final scene (in which Varinia shows Spartacus their son) voted one of the weepiest movie moments of all time.

Throughout her career, Jean Simmons delivered memorable performances both on stage and screen, winning another Oscar nomination for 1969's *The Happy Ending*, and appealing to a new generation with her roles in the television series *The Thorn Birds* and American Civil War drama *North and South*, and giving her vocal talents to the animated movie *Howl's Moving Castle* in 2004, before appearing in *Shadows in the Sun* released in 2008.

'We had to shoot it very, very quickly,' Jean revealed in a 2008 interview with the *Guardian* about working on *Shadows in the Sun.* 'There was no time for retakes or anything like that.' However, despite the tight schedule, she clearly loved being back on a movie set. 'It's the most beautiful place and so healthy with the country air and the sea air,' she said about the movie's location on the Norfolk coast. 'We were all health nuts [on set], drinking green tea all the time. I haven't worked for such a long time. It brought a joy back to my life that I thought I had lost. It personally did me the world of good.'

Jean Simmons died at her home in Santa Monica of lung cancer on 22 January 2010.

Six years after the movie was made, Jamie chatted about working with Jean in an interview with *Interview Magazine*, and it was clear that he was in awe of the actress who had been 79 years old when they met, and had entertained him on set with stories about all the movies she had been in during her career. 'She worked with Marlon Brando and Frank Sinatra – in the same movie! I'm sure she got sick of me asking her about that. She told me one of her first jobs was as Vivien Leigh's stunt double. They rolled her up in a carpet and threw her into a pool for a scene where Vivien was to be drowned. She said she stayed underwater for what to her seemed like forever, but when she came up, she knew it was only a few seconds. She laughed about it, then she went from that to starring in *Spartacus!*'

Jamie loved working with Jean and told the *Scotsman* newspaper how grateful he was to have known her. 'One of my favourite people in the world,' he remembered. 'It was a huge loss when she slipped away. *Shadows in the Sun* was her last film and she was the most incredible person. I kept in touch with Jean and went for lunch at her place in Santa Monica a couple of times. She was hilarious, and had the spirit of a 21-year-old right up to her final days.'

The winner of two awards at the 2009 WorldFest Houston, for Best Screenplay and the Special Jury Award for Best Film, *Shadows in the Sun* was a sweet finale to Jean's career. For Jamie, however, it was to be his last feature film for nearly four years. The bright lights of Hollywood were beckoning, but it was television that was to provide him with his biggest break so far . . .

Once Upon a Time

In 2010, as Jamie was dividing his time between acting auditions, appearances in a couple of shorts (he made *Nice To Meet You* and *X Returns* in 2009, both of which can be found on YouTube) and modelling, rumours were circulating Hollywood that a new fantasy television series, based on classic fairytales, was in the works, and that Adam Horowitz and Edward Kitsis, two of the writers on cult series *Lost*, were behind it. Agents for actors and actresses in Hollywood, New York, Canada and London suggested their clients for lead roles in the show, and one of those mentioned to the producers was Jamie.

The show was titled *Once Upon a Time*, and had actually first been on Horowitz and Kitsis's minds back in 2004, before they joined the writing team on *Lost*. In 2011, Horowitz spoke to Christina Radish at Collider.com about their original idea. 'The idea for the show really started over eight years ago, when Eddie [Kitsis] and I had just come off working on [TV series] *Felicity*. The seed of it was that we were trying to figure out what it is about storytelling that we really love, and what we love is the mystery and excitement of exploring lots of different worlds. Fairytales clicked with us because they were so much in the DNA of what made us storytellers, to begin with.'

The clever idea of *Once Upon a Time* was this – there was a time when all the fairytale characters we know and love really did exist, in an enchanted forest and magical land. Snow White, Prince Charming, Red Riding Hood, Rumpelstiltskin, Belle from *Beauty and the Beast*, Tinker Bell and many others lived there, until the Evil Queen cursed them all to live in our modern world, transported to a New England town called Storybrooke where none of them remember their former selves, their magical powers or their happy endings. In flashbacks, however, the audience sees both their everyday new lives and their former enchanted adventures, too. To complicate the adventure, there is one boy in Storybrooke who thinks he does know the truth about all the people there, and he brings in the mother who gave him up for adoption to help him find out who the residents of the sleepy town really are.

In 2011, Kitsis and Horowitz talked about their ideas to reporters at the Disney D23 fan expo, where new shows are revealed to fans before they are broadcast. 'We came up with the idea that the daughter of Snow White and Prince Charming would come to this small town that was actually the enchanted forest, and there was a curse,' Horowitz told reporters. 'We went out and pitched it to networks and they were like, "Here's this really big idea and it has fairies and dwarves and children and everything you're not supposed to put in a pilot [a pilot is the first episode of a new TV series, that is often broadcast to see if it is successful before any other episodes are made]." They looked at us and said "No way!"'

'When we got on *Lost* we started to realise the way we thought about telling it wasn't right, so it was a good thing it

SHADES OF JAMIE DORNAN

didn't sell,' Kitsis continued. The pair continued to work on the idea, and by 2010 they had ironed out the kinks and were preparing to gather together a cast and crew and put the show together. 'We're interested in either telling the origin stories [of fairytale characters] or the real character things. Like, why is Grumpy grumpy? Why is Geppeto so lonely he carves a little boy out of wood? Why is the Evil Queen evil? To us, that's much more interesting, exploring the missing pieces rather than retelling the story.'

Horowitz added, 'For us, these stories are so well known and they are shared throughout cultures. But with that said, while everyone may know the name Rumpelstiltskin, they may not remember the story completely, and one of our goals for the show is to be able to bring these stories to life to people who may not be as familiar with them.'

After talking to ABC Studios, who would be financing and broadcasting the show, Horowitz and Kitsis set about finding a cast for their series. The main characters they had to find actors for were Snow White (and her 'normal world' alter ego, school teacher Mary Margaret), Emma Swan and Henry (the son she gave up for adoption, who is the first to suspect the residents of Storybrooke may not remember who they really are), the Evil Queen (alter ego Mayor Regina Mills), Prince Charming (aka everyday guy David Nolan), Rumpelstiltskin (aka curiosity shop owner Mr Gold), Red Riding Hood (aka waitress Ruby), Jiminy Cricket (aka psychiatrist Archie Hopper) and the Huntsman (aka Sheriff Graham).

The producers were looking for both American and British actors for the main roles, and Jamie auditioned for the pivotal role of the Huntsman. 'I was in LA doing my first pilot season,' he told *Once Upon a Time*'s spin-off magazine, explaining that is when actors audition for roles in the new shows being produced. While he was being considered, the rest of the cast was beginning to come together, including film and TV actors such as Ginnifer Goodwin, acclaimed Scottish actor Robert Carlyle, Jennifer Morrison and Josh Dallas.

'Everyone we wanted, did it,' Horowitz told Collider.com. 'We went to Ginnifer Goodwin, we went to Jennifer Morrison. We went to Robert Carlyle. We sent them the script and we said, "Would you want to do it?" and they unbelievably all said, "Yes". It was very heartening. For us, with the pilot [episode] there's been this sense of enthusiasm from everyone. Everyone who signed onto the show did so because they wanted to do it, and they're excited about the material.'

Ginnifer Goodwin, playing the dual roles of a tough Snow White and meek school teacher Mary Margaret, was previously best known for her role in the television series *Big Love*, while her long-time friend Jennifer Morrison, who plays Emma, had been a series regular alongside Hugh Laurie on *House*. Scottish actor Robert Carlyle, meanwhile, best known for his film roles in *Trainspotting* and *The Full Monty*, took on the dual role of Mr Gold and Rumpelstiltskin, and shared the screen with former *24* actress Lana Parilla as the Evil Queen and Storybrooke's Mayor, Regina.

Of course, the most interesting casting was Jamie. He told *Once Upon a Time* magazine: 'Now and again, something comes along that you are excited about, your agents are excited about, and there seems to be a lot of buzz about. *Once Upon a Time* was one of those. You work hard for all of them ... but *Once Upon a Time* is one of those that felt like the right thing to put your energy into. Who doesn't love fairytales, you know? And I knew, as I guess a load of people did, about [co-creators] Adam and Eddy before. So it was a whole host of those things that made the project more exciting than the others, and I was lucky to latch onto it.'

He was cast as the Huntsman in the enchanted forest sequences and Storybrooke's sheriff in the real life ones in the summer of 2011. ShowbizOfficial website spoke to Jamie as it was announced he had won the role. 'The premise of the show is to enlighten people about the stories of these characters that we think we already know. We wanted to mess with people's minds and show them a different side to the personalities of the fairytale superstars,' he told them. 'My character [the sheriff] can't be characterised, but I'd say he is edging on the side of the goodies. He's not so easy to work out!'

In the interview, he chatted about the biggest change in his life after accepting a role on the show – a move to Vancouver, where the series is filmed. Many of the forests around the city were used for the magical scenes in the series, while a Vancouver studio was used for the interiors of castles, creepy caves, and magical vaults, thanks to computer trickery that had the actors performing with a green screen behind them with the background effects added in later. However, the town of Storybrooke itself couldn't be created on a screen, so Steveston, a small town not far from Vancouver, doubled for Storybrooke itself. Steveston is best known as a historic salmon-canning centre due to its proximity to the Fraser River, and was named after the first white family to settle in the area in 1877, led by Manoah Steves. It had been used as a filming location before, for the Zac Efron movie *The Death and Life of Charlie St Cloud* in 2010, some episodes of the cult sci-fi series *The X-Files*, and the series *Supernatural*.

With the cast and crew based together in Vancouver, all those involved in the production soon became friends. A romance between Prince Charming and Snow White moved into real life, too, when actors Josh Dallas and Ginnifer Goodwin announced they were a couple off screen as well as on. Jamie, meanwhile, was concentrating on his dual role. His character was the sheriff of Storybrooke, but as the series progressed viewers discovered that he was also the Huntsman, the man sent by the Evil Queen to kill Snow White in the Enchanted Forest.

As the Huntsman, Jamie had to play a pretty mean character who has been raised by wolves and had very little contact with humans, preferring to spend his time with animals. The Huntsman has to do the Evil Queen's bidding, while in Storybrooke, his alter ego, Sheriff Graham is just as under the spell of the Queen as in fairytale land – although in the 'real world' she's the mayor, and to complicate matters even further, Graham is having an affair with her. He does eventually stand up to her though, leading to some of the most fun scenes of the series.

'The joy of this show is that you do have two characters to play and we're conscious of the other one – when you're playing one, you're thinking of the other. He's the victim of bullying by her (the mayor) and everyone wants to have the opportunity to stand up to their bully, so I enjoyed the scenes where I put her back in her place.'

Jamie's two characters unfolded as the series progressed, and viewers learned that his Sheriff Graham is torn between

Regina and a growing crush on new Storybrooke resident Emma. The seventh episode, broadcast in December 2011 in the US, was the one that allowed Jamie to truly shine – titled 'The Heart is a Lonely Hunter', it focused on the sheriff and his alter ego as he realised his feelings for Emma in the real world. 'It was a thrill to play those moments with Jennifer [Morrison, who plays Emma] because she's amazing,' Jamie told *Once Upon a Time* magazine. 'She's a brilliant actress and close friend. By that stage, we had been living in Vancouver for three months and that made everything comfortable, too.'

Completely unaware in early episodes that there is a fairytale land that he is part of, Jamie's character, Graham, gets his first glimpse of it in episode seven when he kisses Emma and has a flashing image of a wolf – a wolf we later discover is the pet of the Huntsman back in the Enchanted Forest. ('They are completely stunning, and they are huge!' Jamie told *Once Upon a Time* magazine about his wolf co-stars, one of which also had a leading role in the *Twilight* movies. 'He at times felt very much like a dog and I almost wanted to wrap my arms around him and hug him, but the reality is he's very much a wild animal.')

Graham later dreams of the wolf and when he tells Mr Gold – the only other resident apart from the Mayor who remembers their other lives – Gold replies: 'They say that dreams . . . dreams are memories. Memories of another life.'

It is just one of the hints in the episode that leads Graham to think he may be someone else. However, as fans of the series know, tragedy awaits him before he can truly discover who he is. Unbeknownst to Graham, the Evil Queen (aka The Mayor) has stolen his heart and keeps it in a vault, ready to squeeze the life out of him anytime she pleases. As Jamie explains: 'In the final scene [of that episode] there is this revelation, this final moment when he realises that he was another person and all his questions come out in that split second. Just when you think it is all coming up daisies, it all gets taken away. The sad part is, also in that split second, Regina (the mayor) crushes the Huntsman's heart that kills the sheriff in Storybrooke as well.'

Yes, just as fans – and Emma – were falling in love with the sheriff's character, he was killed off in the series, just seven episodes in. Fans were in uproar, messaging *Once Upon a Time* chat rooms about how upset they were that the sheriff was dead. 'I think the fact that so many people were upset, I take it as a compliment,' laughed Jamie. 'As deaths go, it was fairly dramatic. Eddy now jokes that he gets threats from hardcore Graham fans, so he's dealing with the aftermath more than I am, I imagine!'

Jamie told E! Online that he'd seen lots of comments about the shocking ending on Twitter. 'People are mad and lovely about it [Graham being killed off] because almost every day I get someone on Twitter saying I should be back, which is very kind and sweet. It makes me feel good and embarrassed at the same time. It's lovely that people care so much. I'd like to say it's all down to me, but it's mostly about the character the writers created.'

'It's pretty gruesome,' he told E! Online, about his character's heart being crushed, 'but you know, it's a little bit cool. Not many people get to die like that. It's a bit cooler than getting shot in the arse or something. So as TV deaths go, I was pretty happy!'

In an interview with Wetpaint Entertainment, Jamie noted that while fans were devastated about the death of Graham, the character of Emma in the show didn't take long to find a new love (she has two potential boyfriends by the end of season two). 'I'm still pretty upset that she [Emma] got over Graham so quickly! You know, I thought we had a couple of nice moments. I died in her arms. You'd think that she'd need a long spell off guys, but she jumped straight back into the saddle.'

Jamie's departure from *Once Upon a Time* led to a glossy eight-page interview in the magazine based on the series, in which he talked about the role and how it was something of a milestone in the series, because his character, Sheriff Graham, was the first major character to die.

In the interview, Jaime admitted he had known the sheriff was going to be killed off even before they had started shooting the series. 'I was just fine with it. To be involved at all in a show like this is pretty cool considering it was the first thing I'd done. I was happy and excited because I liked their plan for the character. They [Eddy and Adam] were so honest with me about the whole process.'

The process included Jamie not knowing who his character's fairytale side was when he signed up for the role. He didn't know that the sheriff was also the Huntsman, and it was clever of the producers to keep Graham's other side a secret, allowing Jamie to focus on the sheriff's job in the town and his connection to the mayor, Regina.

Jamie did try to guess who his fairytale character might be, leading him to do some research on characters such as Robin Hood. 'I knew it had to be a character that had an inner struggle which would have made sense with Graham's power struggle with Regina in terms of his personal life and his professional life in Storybrooke. And then when he was finally confirmed as the Huntsman, I really got into the depths of why he was like he was in Storybrooke.'

He did return for the finale of season one, 'A Land Without Magic', where even more was learnt about his character, and again in the season two episode 'Welcome to Storybrooke', broadcast in the spring of 2013. Filmed in late 2012, almost a year after he left the show, the episode featured flashbacks showing how the characters of the Enchanted Forest, including the Huntsman, had arrived in Storybrooke following the Evil Queen's curse.

'It was kind of really strange,' Jamie told Wetpaint Entertainment, about returning to the set of *Once Upon a Time* after leaving in late 2011. 'It feels like I haven't missed one day filming. It was essentially 90 per cent the same crew and cast, these people I worked with fairly consistently for a good four months. Same location, same faces. In a really lovely way, it was just like coming home to family. In a really eerie way it felt like I hadn't been away.'

Jamie also spoke to the *Huffington Post* about his return to the series, and the support of his *Once Upon a Time* fans. 'It's cool to be considered someone that people want to see more of. It's sort of unexpected for me, I guess as it is for everyone else. That's the beauty of [the series]. There's no definite pattern to anything so the risk or reward of me coming back now and again is quite likely. I love it.'

'It was almost two years ago, to the day, that we were filming the pilot,' he told the *Hollywood Reporter* about filming 'Welcome to Storybrooke'. 'I very much feel like I'm part of the makeup of *Once Upon a Time*. It didn't feel that weird going back, it felt normal. It's kind of bizarre to hang that leather [sheriff's] jacket up and think that's the last time you'll be wearing that, and then, lo and behold, you're back in. It's really sweet.'

Certainly, his character had become a favourite that viewers wanted to see again – and Jamie was even voted 'Hump Day Hottie' by the website Hollywood Crush. 'I'm honestly . . . if you could see me I'm crying from happiness,' he told the site upon learning of the pin-up honour. When the site asked him about his dating life, however, Jamie confessed he wasn't that skilled with the ladies despite now being a TV sex symbol. 'I run away. I promise you,' he said about dating. 'I'm very nervous in that world. Do guys actually use [pick up lines]? Isn't that just in movies?'

He may have joked about his new found status as a sex symbol, but Jamie's next career move would take him far away from life as a heartthrob as he prepared to start the most challenging role of his career . . .

The Fall

A s 2012 began, Jamie was enjoying the success of his role
in *Once Upon a Time* and on the lookout for a new acting
project. The one that was to come along first was far removed
from his heartthrob role in the US television show – it was a
gritty Irish drama about a cop investigating a series of grisly
murders in Belfast.

Written by Allan Cubitt, best known for the series *Murphy's
Law* and *Prime Suspect*, the drama, entitled *The Fall*, was
announced in February 2012. Described by Ben Stephenson,
controller of BBC Drama Commissioning, as 'a unique, foren-
sic and characterful take on a classic genre', the five-episode
drama was to star Gillian Anderson and an as-yet-to-be-cast
Irish actor. All Stephenson would reveal at the time was that
'Cubitt's rich and complex psychological thriller, combined
with another compelling performance from Gillian Anderson,
will keep viewers on the edge of their seats.'

Anderson was the first cast member to be announced in February, with filming due to start in Belfast a month later. She
was a top name for the BBC to have on board their new series,
being best known, of course, for her role in the iconic nineties
sci-fi series *The X-Files*.

Born in Chicago in 1968, Gillian spent the first 15 months of her life in Puerto Rico where her father was working before they relocated to the Crouch End and Stroud Green areas of London where her father attended the London Film School. When whe was 11 years old, the family moved to Grand Rapids, Michigan. Her time in the UK served her well, giving her a British accent that would come in handy in her acting career later in life, but it wasn't always easy growing up and speaking differently to everyone else. 'Even on the phone my accent will change,' she told Nigel Farndale of the *Daily Telegraph*. 'Part of me wishes I could control it, but I can't. I just slip into one or the other. When I moved to the States [as a teenager] I tried hard to cling onto my British accent because it made me different.'

After earning a Bachelor of Fine Arts degree in 1990, Anderson moved to New York and worked as a waitress to make ends meet between acting jobs. After appearing in a drama called *Class of 96*, she was sent the script for a new series called *The X-Files*. A show about two FBI agents, one a believer in the supernatural (Mulder, as played by David Duchovny) and the other a sceptic (Scully, Anderson's role), the series was created by Chris Carter. While TV executives wanted a blond, model-style actress in the lead role, Carter 'fought tooth and nail to get me', Anderson revealed in an interview with the *Chicago Tribune*. She expected the series to run for just 13 episodes, but instead it became a huge hit and ran for nine years, also spawning two movies (1998's *The X-Files* and 2008's *The X-Files: I Want To Believe*).

Over those years, Anderson went from a little-known actress to a huge TV star, winning an Emmy Award for her performance, and also raising eyebrows with the cover shoot she did for men's magazine *FHM* in 1996, that became a landmark cover in the lads' mag market as it depicted an intelligent, sexy woman on the cover rather than a Playboy-style model, and gained her the title 'Sexiest Woman in the World'. 'I remember doing that first interview for *FHM* – I was in Vancouver wearing flannel pyjamas with cowboys on them,' she told the *Telegraph*. 'My hair was messy and I didn't feel sexy at all. I felt exhausted, my daughter was downstairs and there I was being told I was a sex object. I laughed out loud!'

After *The X-Files* ended its run in 2002, more film and TV work followed for Anderson. She won acclaim for her role in the 2000 period drama *The House of Mirth*, and in 2005 was nominated for a BAFTA for her performance in the BBC TV adaptation of Charles Dickens' *Bleak House*. Now living in the UK full-time, she also won praise for her performances in the movie *The Last King of Scotland* with James McAvoy, and the West End theatre production of Ibsen's *A Doll's House*.

By the time her casting in *The Fall*, as Detective Superintendent Gibson, was announced in 2012, Gillian Anderson had also won rave reviews for her performance as Miss Havisham in the BBC's 2011 three-part adaptation of Dickens' classic novel *Great Expectations*, so the press was excited to hear about the role she would be taking on next. Little was revealed, however, until late March when the final announcements were made about the actors who were to appear in the cop drama.

On 26 March 2012, it was announced that Jamie Dornan had taken the lead role alongside Gillian. He was cast as Paul Spector, 'a serial killer who is terrorising the city of Belfast'. Announcements over the following few days added *The Good*

Wife's Archie Panjabi, *Hollyoaks*' Bronagh Waugh and Gerard McCarthy to the cast.

Filming had now begun in Belfast and was scheduled to finish in June 2012. Allan Cubitt talked to the BBC about setting the drama in the Irish city. 'Setting *The Fall* in Belfast and the surrounding area was an easy choice for me. I've always found Northern Ireland a fascinating place, culturally and geographically, and I already had a great working relationship with Stephen Wright [BBC Northern Ireland's Head of Drama] and BBC NI. Having the city as a backdrop – hopefully almost a character in itself – also allowed me to draw on the disproportionate amount of homegrown acting talent there is. I really hope that seeing those actors – some relatively new to the screen – working alongside someone as iconic and potent as Gillian Anderson will make for compelling viewing.'

From the set of the series, Gillian said: 'When I first read the script I had a really strong sense of who she [my character] was and the kind of world that she lives in. The best aspect for me is getting the opportunity to work on a script this good.' She also added, 'This is the first time in a very long time that no matter what, whether it is in the punctuation or in the beats of the scenes that everything is on the page.'

The plot of *The Fall* was this: driven London detective DSI Stella Gibson (Anderson) is drafted from the Metropolitan Police force to review an investigation into a sexually driven murder in Belfast, believed to be the work of a serial killer. Unusually for a thriller, the audience knows who the killer is from the very first episode: a young, good-looking, married family man named Paul Spector (Jamie Dornan) who leads a normal life during the day and is the last person you would suspect of carrying out these brutal killings. The questions that grip viewers over the five episodes is whether DSI Gibson will work out who the killer is, whether she can catch him, and why Paul is driven to kill in the way he does.

It was certainly a change of pace from Jamie's dashing role in *Once Upon a Time*. 'It was hard to find our Paul Spector,' said Julian Stevens, one of the series' producers. 'We had such a clear character in mind and there was no one in our heads who could achieve the balance of the intensity we needed and also the warmth we also needed. Actors came in to read for the part but we didn't feel that we were finding our Spector. We then got Jamie in and it was a revelation. He's an incredibly talented actor and he blew us away and confirmed all our hopes that he was our Spector.'

'We looked at a lot of different new talents, we tried to find a usual suspect to play the killer,' said director Jakob Verbruggen from the set. 'But to find a young and bright person to do that, and I think that Jamie delivers a performance that no one would think a serial killer would give, to be honest.'

In an interview with the *Belfast Telegraph*, writer Allan Cubitt talked about the casting of Jamie. 'There was something very special about Jamie. He's clearly very attractive and we wanted to avoid that cliché that serial killers are men who can't get women. While Jamie might be just starting out, he has the instincts that Gillian [Anderson] has honed over the years, like how to be still and find the beat in every moment. He was a joy to be around. He was very committed to the role and was prepared to do anything asked of him. He's a complete revelation. When he left the room, we knew we'd found our Paul Spector.'

In fact, Jamie had actually auditioned for a smaller part – one of the police investigators, and was astonished when he was called back in and asked if he would audition for the role of Paul. 'I was terrified, bewildered but absolutely flattered to be offered the biggest male part,' he remembered. 'I never think auditions have gone well. But with this one I actually did think I did a good job,' he told Lee Randall of the *Scotsman*. 'Then I didn't hear anything for a couple of weeks. I went to Los Angeles for meetings, and my London agent rang and said they wanted me to come back to read a different part. That usually means it's some tiny, insignificant part, but it was completely the opposite, which never happens.

'I don't know what that says about me – that they saw the serial killer in me?'

On a break from filming, Jamie talked about the part: 'He's an interesting character to play because he has two very distinctive sides to him. What seems like a pretty conventional family existence, he has a wife and two young kids, he's got a good job as a bereavement counsellor, on paper everything looks pretty set and normal. But he also has a different side to him which is that he is evil within this production. I approach him as two different characters, there is an outfit he wears and there is a ritual to it and I find that really helps to become that side of him. I don't find it any harder to lock into than the nice side – it comes more naturally than I had hoped!' he laughed.

'Most of my scenes happen to be with lovely young actresses whom I am doing really brutal things to, and I apologise at the start of the day. They have all been fantastic as it's not an easy thing to subject yourself to but those days when we have had to do those things haven't actually been as harrowing as they are on the page thanks to the crew. They work really hard but it's fun.'

'I think the story of *The Fall* is very intriguing – it's not just about looking for a serial killer, it's also getting to know the killer, it's a killer that lives amongst us,' added Verbruggen about the series. 'He doesn't look like a psychopath, he's not your average killer.'

The story doesn't just focus on Jamie's serial killer character, however. Instead it touches on the lives of the police investigating his crimes, his family, and also the city of Belfast itself where the series is set.

The city is, of course, Jamie's hometown and he talked to journalist J.P. Watson about filming the story of a serial killer there. 'I come from Holywood, a lovely part of the city. Growing up there it was like, "Let's go out shopping in Belfast", "no, bomb scare", "ah, right, fuck it." You got used to that. But with serial killers, none of them have ever come from Belfast. They've come from places in the north of England but we've never had it, which is bizarre. We're very used to murder. Mass murder. But never anything like this [that's in the series].'

When asked whether he was staying with his dad while filming *The Fall*, Jamie laughed. 'Would I stay with him during the shoot? God no. My dad delivers babies. Can you imagine? I've spent all day strangling women, while Dad's bringing a new life into the world. I can't deal with that!'

One thing Jamie did do was prepare for the role before he turned up on set. He had to research serial killers, and particularly those who targeted women, to get into Paul's mindset. In the weeks before filming began, he had very dark books sitting on his bedside table. 'I had to put myself in some pretty awful head space to allow myself to do the role justice,' he told Maureen Coleman of the *Belfast Telegraph*. 'I spent several months reading books about terrible, unspeakable acts carried out by psychopaths. His self-imposed reading homework included such cheery-sounding reads as *Inside the Mind of a Serial Killer* and *Why Men Kill*, to give him some background into why some men carry out murder after murder.

One famous killer in particular striking bore some similarities to the character of Paul Spector: American serial killer Ted Bundy. 'He was a fascinating character, who referred to himself in the third person and did not associate himself with Ted Bundy, the killer. He had a girlfriend, a good job, a great circle of friends, was good looking and bright. But there was this other side to his personality, who carried out unspeakable stuff.'

Ted Bundy was the notorious American serial killer who confessed to 30 murders that he committed between 1974 and 1978 in seven different states. Handsome and charismatic, he won the trust of young women, often feigning a disability or injury when he approached them before overpowering them and abducting them. He performed sexual acts on some of the corpses of the women he killed, decapitated some of them and strangled others. He dumped some of the bodies while keeping others as trophies. He was finally captured in 1978 and in 1980 was sentenced to death by electrocution. He was eventually executed in January 1989.

Jamie watched every interview he could find featuring Ted Bundy, as he told the *Scotsman* in an interview. The notorious murderer is certainly fascinating, as he was apparently a charming man, who carried out his murders while having a girlfriend who never suspected anything, and moved about in society and lived an entirely normal life while performing unspeakable acts that no one knew about. Bundy was easy to compare to Jamie's character of Paul, who has a job and a family, yet is also a serial killer.

Bundy, who was drawn to kill attractive young women, was popular, just like Paul in *The Fall*. 'The thing with Spector is we know after five minutes that he is the killer, so those bits where he is with his children and wife or at work have to be all the more sincere,' Jamie told the *Belfast Telegraph*. 'I had to show that there were characteristics about him that are likeable, endearing. The audience feels some softness towards him during those moments and then when we see the horror of the other side of his personality, there is no sympathy at all.'

To keep things light on the set during the darkest moments of the series, Jamie joked around, realising that it was best to keep things light when the cameras were not rolling rather than take Paul's creepy personality home with him.

His sense of humour led Jamie to become a popular member of the cast during filming, and while they only shared scenes over the telephone, Jamie and Gillian Anderson became friends off set, too, sharing many laughs while they were promoting their series in magazine and newspaper interviews. During an interview with *Red* magazine, the interviewer noticed that the pair joked together, with Gillian offering advice on Jamie's career and reminiscing about his casting. 'They made you jump through some hoops,' she joked. 'But I think it was pretty clear from the beginning that you were the man for the job. I just think it was a matter of convincing the powers that be. I've been in the same situation before, with people fighting my corner, but having to convince studios that you're the one, it takes some effort.'

Jamie agreed, adding that being a former model may have helped him in the US but worked against him in the UK, where it is assumed that if you model, you can't act. Actors such as *Lost*'s Josh Holloway, Charlize Theron, Mark Wahlberg, Ian Somerhalder, Michelle Pfeiffer, Matt LeBlanc and Channing Tatum (who worked as a male stripper before his acting career took off) all started as models but didn't find it hard to move into acting, whereas in Britain, Jason Statham, Tom Hardy and, of course, Jamie, are the exceptions to the rule.

'It's so weird, because my experience is completely opposite,' Gillian replied. 'When I first moved here [to the UK] I was offered *Bleak House* which is so different to anything I'd ever done before. Not in a million years would I have got a role like that in the States. There was a belief here that, even though I'd done Scully, I could do period drama, too. I wanted to say to them, "Why do you think I can do this?"'

'But Scully is a really fucking interesting character, in a massive show, and you're really impressive in it,' replied Jamie. 'So that's nine years of constantly being impressive as an actress, whereas I've got nine years of leaning against walls – and it treated me well, but it was almost to my detriment as an actor.'

Throughout the interview, the pair laughed and joked, with Jamie teasing Gillian that he never had a chance to show her around his native Belfast since she was always sneaking back home to London where her children live. Jamie, meanwhile, took advantage of having three months in Belfast during filming. With many of his friends still living in the city, he got the chance to see all of them and enjoy the busy heart of Belfast as well, staying in an apartment in the middle of town rather than being in the quieter suburbs where he grew up.

While Jamie and Gillian worked on *The Fall* in the spring of 2012, it wasn't until the following May that the BBC broadcast the series. In the meantime, both Gillian and Jamie worked on other projects, but knew they had been part of something special that may just be a hit. They weren't disappointed – on 13 May 2013 *The Fall*'s first episode was broadcast on BBC2 to an impressive audience of 3.5 million viewers – making the series the highest-rated drama launch on BBC2 for almost eight years.

Not only was the show a hit with viewers, it was a hit with critics, too, and deservedly so. Gripping, tense, dark and led by two superb performances from Gillian and Jamie, the series won much praise, with the *Daily Telegraph* describing it as 'an alarmingly intimate portrait of a killer', with Gerard O'Donovan of the newspaper commenting that it had 'a fine beginning and an absolutely stonking end'. Gabriel Tate of *Time Out*, meanwhile, wrote that it was 'beautifully paced, well-sustained and shot half like a dream, half like a nightmare' and Lucy Mangan of the *Guardian* added that the series had 'long, slow tightenings of the dramatic tourniquet until the tension rose almost high enough in viewers' throats to choke them.'

While both Gillian and Jamie's performances were praised in every review, many critics singled out Jamie's performance as especially mesmerising. Hugh David of *Cult TV Times* described it as a 'shock to the system', while the *Huffington Post*'s Caroline Frost talked of Jamie's casting as a "revelation" in a role that was sure to become his breakthrough. Lucy Mangan agreed, saying in her review for the *Guardian* that 'I'm assuming that awards makers are already preparing a "Jamie Dornan" stamp to save themselves time. To play a good guy as well as a bad one is not too difficult – to make the one as compelling as the other, and to make them recognisably the same guy too, as Dornan does when the rage and discipline of the serial killer seep into his dealings with the local thugs, is near miraculous.'

Perhaps the best praise both Gillian and Jamie could get, however, was the news, just a few days after the series was broadcast, that *The Fall* was going to get a second series, with Allan Cubitt once again writing about Detective Superintendent Stella Gibson's pursuit of serial killer Paul Spector.

It was also announced that the series was nominated for Best Mini Series at the BAFTAs, while Jamie was nominated for Leading Actor, in the prestigious company of Dominic West (for his portrayal of Richard Burton in *Burton and Taylor*), Luke Newberry (for *In the Flesh*) and Sean Harris (for the gritty drama *Southcliffe*). More nominations for *The Fall* were to come, at the Broadcasting Press Guild Awards, where Gillian was nominated for Best Actress, Allan Cubitt for the Writer's Award, and Jamie for Breakthrough Performance, and at the Irish Film and Television Awards, where Jamie, the series itself, and the original score were all nominated. Only time would tell whether Jamie would be walking off with one of the coveted prizes as one of the best actors on TV in 2013.

There was one person, however, who, when she first saw Jamie in *The Fall*, didn't love every minute of his time on screen. 'She hadn't seen the third episode, so we watched it the other night,' Jamie told *Culture* magazine. 'She was a little bit wary of me for about half an hour after it finished. I had to win back her trust. I guess I didn't quite realise I was capable of coming across so dark.' And the woman who found Jamie so scary on TV? A lady called Amelia Warner, who, by the time *The Fall* reached our screens in the spring of 2013, was also Jamie's wife . . .

Something About Amelia

Before his acting attracted the attention of the press, Jamie's love life had made headlines due to his previous – and very famous – other half, Keira Knightley. After the success of *Once Upon a Time* and *The Fall*, he was the one who was recognised by passers-by on the street, and in 2012 tabloid photos of Jamie started to include a young actress and singer by the name of Amelia Warner.

Born in Liverpool on 4 June, 1982 to actress Annette Ekblom, best known for her role in the stage production of *Blood Brothers*, and *Emmerdale* actor Alun Lewis, Amelia is also the niece of Hywel Bennett, star of the television series *Shelley*. By the age of six, her parents had split up and Amelia and her mum had moved to London, where she was enrolled at The Royal Masonic School for Girls in Rickmansworth Park, just a few miles from the city. It was a great school choice for the daughter of actor parents – not only does the 225-year-old school have a good drama and performance department, but it has also served as the location for film and television shows over the years, including *Raiders of the Lost Ark* (the scene at Indiana Jones's college where he meets with American intelligence agents and explains what the Ark of the Covenant is),

Inspector Morse, the kids' show *The Demon Headmaster* and *Indiana Jones and the Last Crusade* where it once again doubled for Indy's college.

When she wasn't at school, Amelia was with her mother, often waiting around in television studios and theatre dressing rooms for her to finish work. 'When *Blood Brothers* was going on I'd go backstage every now and again. But she [Ekblom] didn't take me to auditions, she didn't drag me along,' Amelia said in a 2005 interview with the *Observer*. 'It was me and her against the world,' she told the *Evening Standard* about her upbringing, in an interview in 2000. 'It must in some ways have influenced me about acting.' Certainly, her mum encouraged Amelia to become an actress and she won her first role while she was still at school, at the age of 16. It was in an episode of the British television series *Kavanagh QC*, alongside John Thaw as the barrister investigating the death of a doctor's wife. A guest role in an episode of hospital drama *Casualty* followed, along with a small part in the mini series *Aristocrats*, that followed the lives of four wealthy sisters in 18th-century England, as played by Serena Gordon, Anna-Marie Duff, Jodhi May and Geraldine Somerville.

She had certainly caught the acting bug, and told Dark Horizons.com in an interview: 'I've always loved films. Watching films and going to cinemas was always one of my very favourite things to do and just to be able to be part of that and to tell a story really appealed to me.'

Amelia managed to juggle her growing career with her school work, gaining three A-levels and a place at Goldsmiths', the college that boasts Damon Albarn, Damien Hirst, Lucian Freud and artist/director Steve McQueen among its previous students, to study History of Art. However, her career really began to take off and at the age of 17 she was offered the role of young Fanny in 1999's feature film adaptation of Jane Austen's *Mansfield Park*, with Frances O'Connor starring as the grown-up Fanny and Jonny Lee Miller as her cousin Edmund. School was put to one side, and she accepted a role in the TV movie *Don Quixote* that was to be directed by Peter Yates (*Bullitt*, *Breaking Away*) and starred an impressive cast that included John Lithgow, Bob Hoskins, Isabella Rossellini and Vanessa Williams.

It was Amelia's next role, however, that really brought her into the spotlight. She won the role of Simone in the movie *Quills*, directed by Philip Kaufman, who had won acclaim for his movies *The Unbearable Lightness of Being* and *The Right Stuff*. *Quills* was to be the story of the infamous Marquis De Sade's years as an inmate in an insane asylum. Once again, Amelia joined an impressive cast – Oscar-winner Geoffrey Rush was cast as the Marquis, Joaquin Phoenix as the Abbé of the asylum, Kate Winslet as the laundress who has been sneaking the Marquis' writings out of the prison, and Michael Caine as Dr Royer-Collard, who attempts to silence the Marquis. Amelia played Caine's underage wife, Simone, who is assaulted by her husband and eventually runs away with a younger man, to the horror of Royer-Collard.

It meant that the first movie sex scene Amelia acted in would be with Michael Caine, and it was a strange one since filming took place on the day of an eclipse. 'In the middle of this [sex] scene which was really intense, we all ran outside [as it became dark], me and Michael both in these kinds of chiffon nighties,' she told Colin Kennedy of *Empire* magazine.

After such a bizarre event, the pair became friends and talked about Caine's cult movie status, as the star of such movies as *Alfie, Get Carter* and *Mona Lisa*. 'He wouldn't believe that he had this cult cool,' she added. 'The Dispensary – that really cool shop [in Kensington, London] – they have *Get Carter* T-shirts and I showed him, and he was like, "Oh my God, I am cool!"'

Amelia, still 17 when the film was released, was actually too young to see it (it was an 18 certificate) due to the violent and sexual scenes. 'The script I read was a lot more explicit [than the final film],' she told the *Observer*. 'The thing is, I loved the script so much, and my mum read the script as well when I got it, and she loved it. And I guess you just kind of think, well, I'll deal with that later. In the original script there was nudity, which was taken away because I was a minor in America. That was a huge relief.'

The film was a critical success and earned three Oscar nominations following its debut at the London Film Festival in November 2000. It was during the festival that Amelia met actor Colin Farrell, and the two quickly became an item, with Amelia bringing the Irish up-and-coming star along as her date to the *Quills* premieres around the world.

Six years older than Amelia, Dublin-born Farrell was on the brink of becoming a big name himself when he met her. He had appeared as Danny Byrne in the British television series *Ballykissangel*, and by late 2000 was being hotly tipped as a Hollywood star following his performance in Joel Schumacher's Vietnam drama *Tigerland*. Movie offers were flooding in, including *Hart's War* with Bruce Willis, *S.W.A.T* with Samuel Jackson, and *The Recruit* with Al Pacino. Colin and Amelia were seen together at premieres and parties, he had her nickname (Millie) tattooed on his ring finger, and then they stunned their friends and families in July 2001 by announcing they had married on a beach in Tahiti – when Amelia was just 19 years old.

A decade later, in an interview with the *Sun*, Amelia clarified what had really happened on their tropical holiday. 'We didn't actually get married – it's not actually true. I think we've been too polite to deny it. We had a ceremony on a beach in Tahiti that was by no means legal, and we knew it wasn't.'

'It was just a thing we did on holiday,' she added. 'We went shark feeding and then we did that. We booked them both on the activities desk at the hotel. It really wasn't this secret wedding that no one was invited to. It was lovely, it was silly, it was sweet but by no means was it a serious thing and I think my mum thought it was quite funny!'

Unfortunately, Colin and Amelia's relationship didn't last for long after their beach 'wedding'. In an interview years later, Colin said 'too fast, too young' was the reason the pair split just four months later in November 2001, while Amelia told reporter Deidre O'Donovan in 2003 that 'I would have married him for real. We were properly engaged, we had a party with family and everything. But it just didn't work out. I loved him so much and I had the most amazing times of my life with him. He was a fantastic partner, we were together just over a year and we spent just two days apart that whole time.'

In her interview with the *Sun*, Amelia added: 'It was a very intense and passionate relationship. It was heartbreaking when it ended.' While Farrell's star continued to rise with roles in movies such as *Daredevil, Minority Report* with Tom

Cruise, and the Oliver Stone epic *Alexander*, Amelia had plenty of her own work to keep her busy (and to keep her away from tabloid headlines linking her former fiancé to actresses Angelina Jolie and Demi Moore, singer Britney Spears and model Josie Maran). Before she made *Quills*, she had filmed the BBC television series *Lorna Doone*, based on the 19th-century Richard Doddridge Blackmore novel, starring as Lorna herself.

Set in Exmoor during the 17th century, the story introduces us to Lorna, the granddaughter in a family of outlaws, the Doones. She is being forced to marry Carver Doone, but is helped to escape her menacing family by John Ridd, a local farmer. Their fraught romance plays out against the backdrop of the death of King Charles II and the fight for his successor, and had previously been made into a film on four occasions (the most famous being a 1990 adaptation starring Sean Bean). The cast for this TV version also included Aiden Gillen, Richard Coyle and James McAvoy and, when it was broadcast at Christmas 2000, it was a critical hit.

Amelia quickly followed her acclaimed work in *Quills* and *Lorna Doone* with more acting roles. She filmed an episode of the hit television series *Waking the Dead*, the comedy *Take a Girl Like You*, *Love's Brother* (starring Adam Garcia, with whom she was briefly linked in the press) and the horror movie *Nine Lives*. Following nine friends who are spending the weekend in a Scottish country house, but who then start to die mysteriously, the movie was best known for featuring socialite Paris Hilton, and was unfortunately a flop at the box office. More roles in low-budget movies followed, including the ensemble comedy drama *Winter Passing* with Ed Harris

('He scared me to death. He's so lovely, but just the thought of him. And you know, he's so inherently . . . intense. Even when he's chilled out, he's intense,') and Will Ferrell, and the biopic *Stoned*, about the death of Rolling Stone Brian Jones.

By 2005, Amelia had amassed a string of critically praised roles, and she was offered a part in the upcoming sci-fi movie *Æon Flux*, based on the television series of the same name. Charlize Theron took the lead role of a warrior in a future-Earth decimated by a deadly disease, while Amelia was cast as her sister. The film wasn't the box office hit everyone was expecting ('Sometimes you can tell very quickly that something's not going to work. Thankfully I was barely in it,' she told *Empire* magazine), but it led to more roles for Amelia, including the British drama *Alpha Male* with Trudie Styler, and the psychological horror movie *Gone*, filmed in New South Wales and Queensland, Australia. 'She's pretty ballsy,' Amelia told *Empire* magazine about her character in the movie, who realises one of her travelling companions may be a killer. 'There's a bit of screaming, but it's certainly not a cheesy horror movie.'

In an interview with Polly Vernon of the *Observer*, however, she claimed she didn't want the roles to lead to fame and fortune. 'I want to stay below the radar and make good films. I have to be careful, I don't want my life to change. I really don't want to be a movie star.'

The life of a Hollywood star didn't appeal to her either. 'It's so English to hate LA. I'd like to say I love it, but I don't,' she told Vernon. 'It's such a weird place. If it were my choice, I wouldn't spend a day there. Everything shuts at eleven! And everyone thinks they're so crazy and wild and liberal and they're not! So much work goes on there, but so much shit goes on there, too.'

Instead of choosing the California lifestyle, by the end of 2005, Amelia had settled into a flat in Ladbroke Grove, West London, not that far from where her future husband would end up living. 'I'm so excited,' she told Nell Card of *Nylon* magazine about her new home. 'It has huge Georgian rooms, with floor-to-ceiling windows and white walls. It's very girly.' Her boyfriend at the time moved in too, and the pair had some other guests – a family of mice that she talked about in an interview with her fan-website Appreciating Amelia Warner. 'I think [the mice] are gone,' she commented in the 2007 chat. 'My mum got a cat and the cat stayed with me for a week and we haven't seen them since. It's weird, because at first when I had mice I kinda thought it was funny, but after like, a year, it's grated away at my sanity. I've lost all humour about it and I'm genuinely frightened of them now!'

After having such a high profile relationship with Colin Farrell early in her career, Amelia was reluctant to talk about her boyfriend – she would only reveal he was a director – and she made a conscious decision to keep her private life completely away from the public eye. It became harder as she signed on to appear in a big-budget movie adaptation of Susan Cooper's fantasy series of novels for kids and young adults, *The Dark is Rising*.

'I took the script and read it and then went in and read and then got it,' she told Dark Horizons about how she won the role. 'It was kind of really easy. It's a really different thing for me because the films that I've done before this have been much more kind of drama-based character kind of small little films.

So it's definitely not what I would naturally be drawn to. It's probably not the kind of thing that I would normally go and see but I really liked the script and it was really exciting to do something different, something with a huge set, the things going on, and so I really enjoyed it.'

Released as *The Seeker* in some countries and *The Seeker: The Dark is Rising* in others, the movie was Hollywood's attempt to capture the young adult fantasy market following on from the huge success of the Harry Potter movies. Alexander Ludwig stars as Will Stanton, who discovers he has special powers on his 14th birthday. It turns out he is caught in a battle between good and evil, and has to seek out six signs before the evil Rider (Christopher Eccleston) does so – although he does manage to find time to develop a crush on pretty school mate Maggie (played by Amelia Warner) who is dating his older brother.

Loosely based on the second book in Susan Cooper's fantasy series, the film changed much of the story and the setting – the book is actually set in the sixties (while the film is set in the present day) and Will is just 11 in the novel. Amelia's character wasn't in the book at all, and there were other changes author Cooper wasn't happy with when the film went into production at the end of February 2007. Filming took place in studios in a remote part of Romania, with Amelia joined on set by her fellow cast members. 'I've been kind of lucky, I've been in and out doing small bits,' she told Cinema.com about shooting in Romania. 'The longest I have been here has been two weeks. It's been strange, because it's half a Romanian crew and half an American crew – the dynamic is quite strange!'

Amelia got on with her co-stars, including British actor Ian McShane ('it was light relief, it was just humour, and not being so earnest and serious about everything. Silly games on set, it was really nice') and she also managed to avoid a scene in which McShane is covered with hundreds of snakes ('they have an albino cobra – they are really warm when you feel them!')

When filming finished three months later, Amelia gave an interview to Cinematical website about the movie, but wasn't able to reveal a great deal! 'I'm not really allowed to say very much about her [Maggie] – she's kind of like a mystery. You don't really know what side she falls on, and in the story, she appears to be a new girl at the school. The character of Will sees her in the village and kind of develops a crush on her, and she's just kind of lingering around. But she's there to look after Will and to make sure that nothing bad happens to him, and she's going to protect him.'

It was an odd experience for Amelia to do publicity for a movie without being able to reveal too much about her role or the plot itself (even though fans of the books already had a pretty good idea of what was going to happen). 'It's really frustrating,' she told Dark Horizons. 'I'm just terrified that I'm going to say something wrong. Those who have read the book will already know kind of who's good and who's bad and the general gist of things. So it's out there.'

Amelia was certainly aware how lucky she was to be appearing in the movie. 'It's a crazy business [to be an actor] because it's something ridiculous like three per cent of actors are actually working, and so any job you get you have to feel lucky and kind of thankful to get it because it's hard, but then you also want to try and pick stuff carefully. It's tough, but I feel very lucky. I'm just very happy if I can continue to do that.'

As soon as she had finished filming the movie in June, Amelia was already lining up her next role in the horror film *The Echo*. Filming began in August 2007 in Toronto, and while on set she gave an interview to her fan-website, Appreciating Amelia Warner, about making a horror movie. 'It's all about the scare, it's about making the moment real,' she said. 'It's quite weird because you don't know how you would react really if you do see something frightening. I don't know what I would do, I think I would just freeze which is probably not very interesting!'

The Echo was based on a Filipino movie called *Sigaw* (both versions directed by Yam Laranas) and told the story of what happens when a young ex-con moves into an apartment building in New York and starts hearing strange noises, finds blood in his apartment, and has visions about the family in the apartment next door. Jesse Bradford starred as Bobby, the ex-con, while Amelia had second-billing as his girlfriend, who is put in danger by the threat in the apartment.

Unfortunately, both *The Seeker: The Dark is Rising* and *The Echo* underperformed at the box office, but by the following year, Amelia's career had moved in a different direction entirely, as she had decided acting was no longer for her. 'It wasn't fulfilling,' she told the *Daily Telegraph*. 'You have no control, there is no responsibility, you go to the audition, and you either get the part or you don't – that's as much choice as you have. Then a year later you see the end product and you can be in a completely different film from the one you thought you were making. It started to get really frustrating.'

Leaving film behind, she began a music career, singing under the name Slow Moving Millie – a name given to her by her friends. 'I was an actress for quite a long time,' she explained to journalist Robert Copsey a few years later in 2011, 'and I wasn't particularly happy doing it. I'd write music just for myself, and my friends were always on at me to take it further. I probably am a bit lazy too, though. I also liked the safety of writing and releasing music under a different name.'

Her first release was the song 'Beasts', which was used in a Virgin Media advert before being released as a single in August 2009 ('after the Virgin deal I finally got some money behind me to leave acting and leap into the music properly' she told Digital Spy website), and she followed it with the single 'Rewind City', that was also used in a commercial, this time for Orange UK. It was her third single, however, that brought Amelia – or Slow Moving Millie – to public attention. It was a cover of The Smiths' 1984 song 'Please, Please, Please, Let Me Get What I Want', which was originally the B-side to their hit 'William, It Was Really Nothing'. The song had been covered numerous times before by acts including Franz Ferdinand, Muse, Hootie & the Blowfish, Deftones and had appeared on the soundtrack for films like *Pretty in Pink* and *Ferris Bueller's Day Off*, but it was Amelia's version that was chosen by John Lewis to be the soundtrack to their Christmas 2011 advert on British television.

'It was my manager who got me involved with the John Lewis ad,' Amelia told Digital Spy. 'It was a situation where they knew what song they wanted and had sent it out to lots of different artists. I was recording a covers album anyway, and my manager asked me to try it out without telling me what it was for. It was about two months later when I found out it was being used for the advert.'

John Lewis had already boosted the careers of other artists by featuring their cover versions of well-known songs in previous Christmas adverts – most notably Ellie Goulding the year before with her version of Elton John's 'Your Song', which became a huge hit. 'It's definitely a good break [to be featured in the ad] and it can be a great platform,' Amelia continued. 'There are so few opportunities in the industry now, and this is a great way to get your music out to as many people as possible. The John Lewis ad is also like the holy grail of ads and it's a great company to be associated with.'

The advert itself was a weepie – following a little boy, bored and impatient as he waits for Christmas. When he wakes up on Christmas Day, he ignores the presents placed at the foot of his bed and instead goes into his wardrobe and brings out a clumsily wrapped present that he delivers to his mum and dad. So did it make Amelia cry? 'I've seen it a lot so I'm immune to it now, but the first time I saw it, I did cry! That little boy is so cute! He's fantastic.'

Just a week after the advert was first launched in November 2011, it had been viewed on YouTube over a million times. People took to Twitter in their thousands to claim it was the most moving advert ever, while others disagreed and said that the despairing ballad, written by The Smiths' lead singer, Morrissey, and Johnny Marr, had been turned into a celebration of consumerism (one fan wrote that it was a 'serious crime against music'). 'I haven't been spat at by Smiths' fans in the street,' Amelia told Neil McCormick of the *Daily Telegraph* when the song was released. 'I've had a few people being furious at me on Twitter saying, "How dare you?" but I haven't done anything to the original. I think you'll find it still exists.'

The song was to form part of her album *Renditions*, which was a compilation of cover versions of pop hits from the eighties.

The album included Amelia's versions of Fiction Factory's 'Feels Like Heaven', and slowed-down versions of Yazoo's 'Don't Go', Frankie Goes To Hollywood's 'The Power of Love', Tears For Fears' 'Head Over Heels', Thompson Twins' 'Hold Me Now' and even Bananarama's 'Love in the First Degree'.

'I was writing my debut album of original stuff and the covers thing was a side project,' she told Digital Spy. 'I'm randomly drawn to songs from that era because I think they often get a really bad rap. A lot are really beautiful songs but because they were written in the eighties . . . a lot of great ballads suffered from overeager producers. I love all of the originals, but they shouldn't have that guilty pleasure label.

'I remember some of the label were concerned about me covering Bananarama because they thought no one would take it seriously,' Amelia continued. 'I think they [the songs] work, and I don't think it should matter who did them originally or whether it's cool or not.'

The John Lewis advert meant that Amelia's cover of The Smiths' song got her a lot of airplay, and the album went on to appear in the Top 100 album chart in the UK. But what Amelia hadn't mentioned in her interviews promoting her music career was that her home life had undergone as big a change as her career – and she was now dating Jamie Dornan.

With both of them having had high-profile relationships in

Jamie launches an international Calvin Klein event in 2009. (Julian Makey/REX)

Left The ever-stylish Jamie attends the British Fashion Awards in 2006. (Richard Young/REX)

Right Posing for photographs on Oxford Street, London. (PA)

Below Sons of Jim perform at the Cobden Working Men's Club in Kensal Green, London. (Steve Parsons/PA)

Left Looking dapper, arriving at a fragrance launch party in 2007. (Getty Images)

Above Jamie and his wife Amelia at the 2014 GQ Men of the Year Awards.
(Getty Images)

Left Snapped on the red carpet, Jamie arrives at a Moet & Chandon event in London. (Corbis)

Above Model behaviour for Calvin Klein. (PA)

Looking suave in Soho, London. (Tony Buckingham/REX)

the past, Jamie and Amelia fiercely guarded their privacy in their new romance. While you can find numerous photos on-line of Amelia with Colin Farrell when they were dating, and of Jamie and Keira Knightley from when they were a couple, search the internet for pictures of Amelia and Jamie together and you will find very few from the early years of their rela-tionship. It's not until an interview in 2013 about *The Fall* that Jamie mentions Amelia (and then, not by name) and the first widely circulated photos of them as a couple emerged when they took a holiday to Miami together at the beginning of that year. In an interview with the *Daily Telegraph*, Jamie talked about his growing celebrity status and wanting to keep his life private. 'Nobody sane just wants to be famous,' he said, 'I hate it when people say you're asking for it by doing films. No, I'm asking for work, and I'm asking to get paid for doing some-thing I love. I'm not asking to be followed down a street by some f**king pap.'

Photographed by the paparazzi or not, by 2013, Jamie was already enjoying pin-up status following his role in *Once Upon a Time* and even *The Fall* (despite him playing a serial kill-er!), so there were many fans who were excited and probably jealous to hear the news that he and Amelia had become en-gaged. And on 26 April 2013 came the news that Amelia had become Mrs Dornan in a quiet ceremony at a country house in Somerset. In keeping with the couple's bid for privacy, it was one of the few celebrity weddings kept under wraps, with no photos appearing on the internet of the bride and groom, despite some high-profile guests being in attendance, includ-ing Jamie's *Once Upon a Time* co-stars Ginnifer Goodwin and Josh Dallas.

There was more exciting news to come. Just two months after their wedding, Jamie and Amelia announced that they were expecting their first child together. With both Jamie's dad and his stepmother working in gynaecology and obstetrics, it came as no surprise when they announced who had performed Amelia's first pregnancy scan. 'Jim [Jamie's dad] and I are delighted that our third grandchild is on the way,' said Samina Dornan to *Sunday Life* in Northern Ireland. 'The early wellbeing scanning was a beautiful and emotional experience for all present.' The scan took place at the 3fivetwo Healthcare clinic in Lisburn Road in Belfast by Samina, who is Consultant Sub-Specialist in Maternal Fetal Medicine at the Royal Maternity Hospital nearby.

'It's a new challenge and adventure, and I can't wait,' Jamie told the *Daily Telegraph* about the forthcoming addition to his family. 'You might sleep a bit less but you've got this small life to look after and I am quite good on little sleep.'

It was unlikely, however, that Jamie and Amelia would be in Ireland for the birth of their child, due at the end of 2013, for just a few months after Amelia learned she was pregnant, Jamie was offered the role of a lifetime. It was a role that would take them both far away from his hometown of Belfast, across the Atlantic Ocean to Vancouver, and turn him from a respected working actor into a worldwide pin-up . . .

Mr Grey Will See You Now

Back in 2008, a series of novels was outselling everything else on bookshop shelves. The four *Twilight* books by Stephenie Meyer – about an American teenager called Bella who falls in love with 104-year-old vampire Edward – were a publishing phenomenon, selling more than 120 million copies worldwide and spawning four hit movies. The books attracted millions of fans, some of whom wrote fan fiction (stories written by fans featuring the characters that they love) about Edward and Bella. One of those fans was a woman named Erika Mitchell, who wrote a *Twilight* fan fiction story entitled *Master of the Universe* under the pseudonym Snowqueen's Icedragon.

Nowadays, people will know Mitchell by the pen name she adopted in 2011 – E.L. James. And that *Twilight* fan fiction called *Master of the Universe*? Well, it's better known as the basis for her first novel, *Fifty Shades of Grey*. The story of a romance – and S&M sexual relationship – between businessman Christian Grey and young Anastasia Steele, it's now one of the most successful books of all time.

In an interview with Deadline.com, Mitchell's book agent Valerie Hoskins remembers how *Master of the Universe* grew into something that became the hottest novel of 2011. 'Originally it was written as fan fiction, then Erika decided to take it down after there were some comments about the racy nature of the material. She took it down and thought, "I'd always wanted to write. I've got a couple of unpublished novels here. I will rewrite this thing, and create these iconic characters, Christian and Ana." If you read the books, they are nothing like *Twilight* now. It's very 21st century, don't you think?'

All of Erika Mitchell's *Twilight* fan fiction that formed the basis of *Fifty Shades* has been removed from the internet, but those who were lucky enough to read *Master of the Universe* have debated, on numerous websites, the similarities, between it and the *Twilight* books it is based on and *Fifty Shades*. For example, the leading man of *Fifty Shades*, Christian Grey, is adopted like Edward Cullen in *Twilight*. He and Edward both give their heroine a car, they are both piano players, they both have a dark secret that only the heroine knows about, they are both rich, and they both fall for girls who are pretty, but awkward (Bella in *Twilight*, Ana in *Fifty Shades*).

Of course, that is where the similarities end, as while *Twilight* was aimed at the young adult market of teenage girls, *Fifty Shades of Grey* is an erotic novel for adults that features S&M and explicit sexual situations. Now a series of three novels (*Fifty Shades of Grey*, *Fifty Shades Darker* and *Fifty Shades Freed*), Erika Mitchell's writing does have one other thing in common with the *Twilight* novels that inspired them – the *Fifty Shades* series has topped bestseller lists around the world, has sold over 100 million books worldwide, and its author was offered millions for her words to be translated into a blockbuster movie.

Certainly, by the end of 2011, Erika Mitchell – or, to be accurate, her pen name E.L. James – was the name on everyone's lips, as *Fifty Shades of Grey* raced to the top of the bestseller lists and became the fastest selling paperback of all time. Soon everyone wanted to know who had written this phenomenon, and it turned out that Mitchell was a mum in her late forties, living in London, who worked as a TV producer. In 2010, when she was still writing as Snowqueen's Icedragon, she wrote on her website: 'I live in West London. I have two boys, a grumpy hubs who betas my work and a West Highland terrier called Max.'

Her biography continued: 'I am old enough to know better, but will try anything once – except incest or folkdancing . . . actually, I've tried folkdancing and it's a hoot. I work in TV – at the moment for an independent television production company based in a small village that could be from The League of Gentlemen (nuff said). We make mainly comedy shows – and it's a lot of fun.'

She went on to explain that she had started writing back in January 2009, after finishing reading the *Twilight* saga, and had posted her fan fiction on fanfiction.net eight months later.

Little did she know how much her life would change with the publication of *Fifty Shades of Grey*. The daughter of a Chilean mother and a Scottish father who was a cameraman for the BBC, Erika Mitchell led a suburban life in Buckinghamshire, attending private school and then the University of Kent, before becoming a studio manager's assistant at the National Film and Television School in London. It was there she met her husband Niall, a scriptwriter best known for television series such as *Hornblower*, *Silent Witness* and *Wire in the Blood.* They married in 1987 and had two sons, and it was Niall who bought her the four *Twilight* books that eventually inspired her to write *Fifty Shades of Grey.* 'I loved, loved, loved them,' she told the *Daily Mail* in 2012. 'I read them in five days [over Christmas] and started writing [fan fiction] in the January.'

In January 2011, Erika signed a print-on-demand and e-book contract with a small Australian publisher called The Writer's Coffee Shop. Her first *Fifty Shades* book that had evolved from the fiction *Master of the Universe* was published in May of that year with the sequel, *Fifty Shades Darker*, following in September 2011. Word of mouth, especially in the USA, meant that e-book sales were rising. 'That was the weird thing — the way it spread,' she told the *Mail.* 'I had no idea it would happen like that.' By Christmas 2011, *Fifty Shades* was trending on Twitter, and Erika spotted one tweet by an executive producer of *The Letterman Show* in New York. 'He wrote: "This Sunday, the guys all watched the football, the women were all reading *Fifty Shades*."

'It's completely and utterly overwhelming,' she added. 'I just wanted to tell a rollicking good story — peppered with lots of sex. I always had vague hopes of being published, but everyone always tells you it won't happen.'

By early 2012, publishing companies were falling over each other to become the one chosen to turn Erika Mitchell's – or, as she was now known, E.L. James' – e-books into print novels and, in March 2012, she signed a lucrative book deal with Vintage.

So why did the *Fifty Shades* trilogy become such a publishing phenomenon? On the face of it, it's an unlikely Mills &

Boon style romance between a millionaire – Christian Grey – and an awkward young woman – Anastasia Steele – set in the city of Seattle, but the reason that the books have become the topic of TV discussion shows, the subject of numerous newspaper think pieces and the one book seemingly every woman has read is the raunchy sex scenes that are sprinkled throughout the books. Christian Grey, you see, has eclectic sexual tastes involving dominance and submission, bondage and discipline, submission and sadism and masochism. In his apartment, he's even got a special room – which Ana dubs the 'red room of pain' – especially for the games he likes to play with his lovers.

James was flooded with letters and tweets from fans thanking her for writing the books. 'One older woman sent me an email saying: "You're waking the dead here," she told the *Daily Mail*. 'Another woman wrote and said: "You've spiced up my marriage. My husband wants to thank you, too."'

It wasn't the first raunchy book ever to be published, of course. D.H. Lawrence's *Lady Chatterley's Lover*, first published in 1928, was not available in an unedited version in the UK until 1960 due to its depictions of sex and use of then-unprintable swear words, and it was even the subject of an obscenity trial. Meanwhile in the sixties, readers were shocked by author Jacqueline Susann's depictions of sex and drugs in the bestselling *Valley of the Dolls*. In the seventies and eighties, it was the novels of Jackie Collins that were on every woman's bedside table, titles such as *The World is Full of Married Men*, *The Stud*, *The Bitch* and *Hollywood Wives*. They were banned in some countries and described by romance novelist Barbara Cartland as 'nasty, filthy and disgusting'. By the mid-eighties, everyone was reading Shirley Conran's *Lace* to find out exactly what part a goldfish plays in one described sex act, and even old-fashioned romantic novel publisher Mills & Boon got in on the sex stuff by launching raunchier imprints such as Blaze, Desire and Spice to appeal to readers who wanted to read about what naughtier things happened after milady had a kiss with the stable boy behind the potting sheds.

There had been novels featuring BDSM (bondage, discipline, sadism, masochism) well before it was featured in *Fifty Shades of Grey*, too, but none aimed squarely at everyday female readers who wanted romance as well. Previously, you would have had to choose from *The Story of O*, the Marquis De Sade's novel *Justine* or Elizabeth McNeill's memoir *9½ Weeks* (later made into the film of the same name), but none of them featured sex and romance in the way that *Fifty Shades* did, successfully combining a Cinderella love story between Ana and Christian with explicit sex and bondage scenes that would be discussed in book clubs around the world.

As mums passed copies of the books to each other in the playground – the popularity of the *Fifty Shades* novels among 30- and 40-something women led to the books being labeled 'mummy porn' – *Fifty Shades* became the two words on everyone's lips. In an interview, Mitchell discussed how she came up with the idea that was ultimately far removed from the *Twilight* fan fiction she had started with: 'I start off with a very simple premise. In the case of the *Fifty Shades* trilogy my premise was, "What would happen if you were attracted to somebody who was into the BDSM lifestyle, when you weren't?"'

She continued: 'I often have a loose timeline to work with, but I don't feel bound to it – I let the characters dictate what happens. I often listen to music to evoke a mood – I will listen to the same song over and over again when I am lost in a scene. Also, I'm obsessed with the geography – i.e. where everything is in a particular room, and the choreography of scenes – whose hand goes where when! And I like to have a visual reference for everything.'

Mitchell, as her pseudonym E.L. James, did receive some criticism for the series of novels. Salman Rushdie said: 'I've never read anything so badly written that got published. It made *Twilight* look like *War And Peace*,' while a *New York Times* review said it was written 'like a Brontë devoid of talent'. There were debates about whether the novel perpetuated violence against women, and complaints from the BDSM community that the dominant relationship was not portrayed properly, and that in real life there is trust between the partners that isn't present in *Fifty Shades*.

Such criticisms – and the banning of the novel in some libraries – didn't stop sales of the book and its two sequels from reaching the millions and propelling E.L. James into the bestseller lists, and *Time* magazine naming her one of the 100 Most Influential People in the World. Even Stephenie Meyer, the author of the *Twilight* books, was impressed by Erika Mitchell's success. 'I haven't read it. I mean, that's really not my genre, not my thing,' she told *MTV News* with a laugh. 'I've heard about it; I haven't really gotten into it that much. Good on her — she's doing well. That's great!'

Fifty Shades had something else in common with Meyer's bestselling *Twilight* books, too – thanks to the success of the steamy trilogy, everyone wanted to talk to E.L. James about translating her pages onto the big screen.

Deadline.com reported in March 2012 that ten movie studio chiefs were rumoured to have been battling it out to win the film rights to *Fifty Shades of Grey* over one frantic weekend. The *LA Times* confirmed that 'over the last few days, top executives from Warner Bros., Sony Pictures, Fox 2000, Universal and Paramount have – or will – deliver presentations, some of them highly elaborate, to convince James and her literary agent Valerie Hoskins that they are the best candidates to transform the popular material into a movie.' It was rumoured one pitch featured a video of female studio employees responding positively to the novels (whatever that means!), while Warner Bros president of production Greg Silverman went after the movie rights after his wife and mother-in-law raved about the books to him. Actor Mark Wahlberg's production company was also interested in making the movie, as he told TV show *Access Hollywood*. 'We were very close to getting the rights, we were talking with the writer before she had an agent. I just knew that it was going to be a phenomenon, whether I thought it was good, bad or indifferent. It was definitely going to be one of those things that would create a huge buzz.' (He did, however, add that he would not have put himself forward for the lead role of Christian Grey because 'I don't think my wife would like that!')

When considering which studio should turn her *Fifty Shades* characters into movie flesh and blood, E.L. James and her agent Valerie Hoskins asked something Hollywood didn't expect of a first-time writer – they wanted E.L./Erika to have final approval over director, cast, locations, trailer and who would write the screenplay for the movie, a request described as 'exceptional' by industry magazine the *Hollywood Reporter* (only established authors such as Stephen King or John Grisham have even half the sway Erika wanted). As a deal was ironed out with Universal Pictures and Focus Features, reportedly for $5 million, news of their stipulations reached Hollywood, and author Bret Easton Ellis (best known for his own controversial novels *American Psycho* and *Less Than Zero*) was one of the first people to offer his assistance.

'I'm putting myself out there to write the movie adaptation of *Fifty Shades of Grey*', he tweeted, but his message was ignored and in October 2012 it was announced that Kelly Marcel, best known as the screenwriter for the family drama about Walt Disney, *Saving Mr Banks*, would write the script for *Fifty Shades*. 'Kelly's work demonstrates her flawless structural technique and passionate commitment to emotion, humor and depth of character, which is particularly visible in the celebrated screenplay for *Saving Mr Banks*,' said producer Michael De Luca, while co-producer Dana Brunetti added: 'We were all taken with the depth and passion of Kelly's engagement with the characters and world E.L. James has created, and we knew she was the right person to augment our *Fifty Shades* family.'

Later, two more writers would be brought in – Patrick Marber, Oscar-nominated for *Notes on a Scandal*, was hired to do a 'character polish' according to the *Hollywood Reporter* before filming began while screenwriter Mark Bomback, best known for *Live Free or Die Hard*, *The Wolverine* and *Dawn of the Planet of the Apes* was also hired to polish the script. Both men had experience of raunchier movies – Marber had written the play and movie *Closer*, which had starred Julia Roberts and Clive Owen, while Bomback was the writer behind the steamy drama *Deception*, which starred Ewan McGregor, Michelle Williams and Hugh Jackman.

With producers and a writer in place, speculation began to mount about the movie. Who would direct the film? Who would star as Anastasia and Christian? And, perhaps most importantly, how would the infamous erotic novel featuring scenes of bondage and explicit sex be brought to the screen without being pornographic?

Of course, Hollywood is no stranger to sex, but including graphic love scenes can make a movie, and its stars, notorious. Sometimes this is a good thing – more people go and see the movie to see what all the fuss is about – but sometimes it can have the opposite effect, with people staying away, too embarrassed to buy a ticket to the eyebrow-raising movie of the moment. And the career paths of actors who had in the past quite literally exposed themselves on film must have crossed the mind of every potential Christian and Anastasia as actors lined up to audition for roles. Would starring in this erotic movie give an actor's career a boost, as *Basic Instinct* did for Sharon Stone and Michael Douglas? Or could it seriously damage their prospects, as *Showgirls* did for Elizabeth Berkley?

Looking at some of the most controversial movies of recent years, it's hard to predict the outcome. Some raunchy movies such as *Basic Instinct* and *9½ Weeks* have become hits, while others – despite well-known stars in lead roles – have flopped at the box office. As just about every actor and actress under 40 was considered for the roles of Christian and Anastasia, perhaps some of those in the frame contemplated the movies that had gone before, and whether it would be a boost to their career or a blot on their CV if they won the part:

Basic Instinct

In 1992, Michael Douglas was a Hollywood megastar, having won an Oscar for his performance in *Wall Street*, and he had earned box office success in movies such as *Fatal Attraction* and *Romancing the Stone*. In director Paul Verhoeven's erotic thriller about a cop investigating a possible murderer, he was teamed with young actress Sharon Stone, who was best known for a minor role in *Total Recall*. Together they made a movie that became one of the highest grossing of the year, and the most controversial thanks to the explicit sex scenes (the film was originally rated NC-17 in the US but after 40 seconds were cut, it was given an R rating), and graphic violence. While Stone has since understandably complained that the infamous leg-crossing scene was filmed without her being aware that the camera was focused up her skirt, both she and Douglas scored many successes after appearing in the hit movie, including his performances in *Falling Down*, *Traffic* and *The Game*, and hers in *Casino*, *Sphere* and *The Mighty*.

Showgirls

Director Paul Verhoeven, who had got it so right with *Basic Instinct*, unfortunately got it very wrong three years later with this 1995 story of a young stripper in Las Vegas who wants to make it as a showgirl. Cheesy dialogue, bad performances (especially from lead Elizabeth Berkley) and a weak plot – it was rumoured scriptwriter Joe Eszterhas scribbled the idea for the movie on a napkin and was offered $2 million to turn it into a script – didn't help the film at the box office. The rating the film was given was also blamed for the movie flopping – it was classified NC-17 in the US which means no one under 17 can be admitted (usually, sexy or violent movies get the less restrictive R that allows younger viewers to be admitted with an adult). Berkley – who accepted a role turned down by Drew Barrymore, Pamela Anderson and Angelina Jolie and won Worst Actress and Worst New Star Golden Raspberry awards for her trouble – has since appeared in minor roles in movies and made guest appearances in television series, including the US dance contest *Dancing with the Stars*.

Shame

Turner-Prize-winning artist Steve McQueen made his feature-length directorial debut with the 2008 movie *Hunger*, and followed it with this acclaimed movie that won the 'CinemAvvenire' Award for Best Film at the Venice Film Festival in 2011. It reunited him with his *Hunger* leading man Michael Fassbender, and explores sexual addiction, telling the story of a successful advertising executive and his various encounters with women and men in New York. Despite the dreaded NC-17 rating in the US for explicit sex scenes and Fassbender's nudity, the movie has been deservedly acclaimed and certainly the sex scenes have done no damage to Fassbender's or McQueen's careers – both went on to make the Oscar-winning *12 Years a Slave*, and Fassbender's subsequent roles have also included blockbusters *Prometheus* and *X-Men: Days of Future Past*.

9½ Weeks

One of the most famous erotic dramas of all time, this Adrian Lyne-directed movie from 1986 is best known for the 'fridge scene' in which businessman Mickey Rourke blindfolds art gallery assistant Kim Basinger and teases her with the various contents of his refrigerator. Like the erotica in *Fifty Shades of Grey*, this scene – and other scenes of sexual role-play – became a talking point, and helped make the movie a hit, especially on video, to the tune of over $100 million. Not bad for a film that got a thumbs down when it was first screened to 1000 people – reportedly only 40 stayed to the end of the film and of those, 35 said they hated it. While it didn't hurt Basinger's career – she went on to star in *Batman* and win an Oscar for *LA Confidential* – Rourke fared less well, starring in a series of box office flops (including a dire *9½ Weeks* sequel called *Another 9½ Weeks*) before quitting acting in order to pursue a boxing career. He has since returned to movies, appearing in *Iron Man 2* and winning praise for his role in *The Wrestler*.

Striptease

By 1996, *Ghost* actress Demi Moore was best known in the tabloid press for the changes she had made to her body – both by exercise and cosmetic surgery – and she showed the results off in this drama based on the Carl Hiaasen novel of the same name. Her character becomes a stripper to earn money, and crosses paths with a shady congressman (Burt Reynolds) who is being investigated by the police. Demi was paid a then-record $12.5 million for her role in a film that would become notorious for its bad performances and awful script (it won six Golden Raspberry awards, including Worst Actress), but a series of flops followed for the actress, and she has made only a handful of little-seen movies since.

Eyes Wide Shut

Reclusive Stanley Kubrick directed this sexual drama that reunited then husband and wife Tom Cruise and Nicole Kidman on screen – they had previously co-starred in the far tamer racing car adventure *Days of Thunder* and Irish period drama *Far and Away*. A confusing, meandering drama about a young couple in New York, the film became well known for an orgy scene, especially after it was digitally altered for the US release (graphic sexuality was blocked out by other figures and objects obscuring the view) and for the frank dialogue between Cruise and Kidman's characters. ('When she is having her little titties squeezed, do you think she ever has any fantasies about what handsome Dr Bull's dickie might be like?') It didn't harm their careers – Kidman went on to make *Moulin Rouge, The Others, Cold Mountain* and *Australia* and Cruise has had numerous blockbuster hits including three *Mission Impossible* films. Their marriage didn't survive, however, with the couple divorcing in 2001.

In the Cut

An erotic thriller based on the Susanna Moore novel, *In the Cut* stars Meg Ryan as a woman, Frannie, who becomes involved with a police detective (Mark Ruffalo) who is investigating the murder of two women – one of whom's limbs were found in Frannie's garden. But the plot was secondary to the audience's shock at Ryan's sex scenes – after all, she was best known for romantic comedies like *When Harry Met Sally* – especially as she appeared naked in one lengthy scene, her first nude scene in a movie. It became the first in a series of flops for Ryan, whose last movie role was in 2009. Ruffalo, on the other hand, has had a string of successes since this movie, including *Collateral, Zodiac, The Kids Are All Right* (for which he was nominated for an Oscar) and *The Avengers.*

Nymphomaniac

A two-part movie from Lars von Trier, released in 2014, this arthouse sexual drama charts a woman's erotic journey from childhood to the age of 50. Charlotte Gainsbourg stars alongside Stellan Skarsgård, Uma Thurman and Willem Dafoe, but it was rumours of actor Shia LaBeouf's full frontal nudity and stories that the sex scenes weren't simulated that made the film newsworthy, months before its release. LaBeouf himself fuelled the rumours in an August 2012 interview with *MTV News*, saying, 'There's a disclaimer at the top of the script that basically says we're doing it for real. Everything that is illegal, we'll shoot in blurred images. Other than that, everything is happening . . .' It was eventually revealed that the sex scenes were filmed using body doubles for the actors, ('We shot the actors pretending to have sex and then had the body doubles, who really did have sex, and in post [production] we will digitally impose the two. So above the waist it will be the star and below the waist it will be the doubles,' explained producer Louise Vesth) and the film went on to receive critical praise for the story and performances.

Women in Love

D.H. Lawrence's classic novel was adapted into a 1969 romantic drama by director Ken Russell – a man who was no stranger to controversy in his career, having made movies such as *The Devils* and the rock opera *Tommy*. Alan Bates and Oliver Reed play the two friends who become involved with the sisters played by Glenda Jackson and Jennie Linden, and the nude wrestling scene between the two male actors was considered shocking enough for the film to be banned in Turkey. While Jennie Linden didn't pursue a Hollywood career after the release of the controversial, and successful, film, Alan Bates continued to give acclaimed performances in movies like *The Go-Between* and *Gosford Park* (he was knighted in 2003 and sadly died later that year), renowned hellraiser Oliver Reed had a varied acting career until his death in 1999, and Glenda Jackson went on to win an Academy Award for her role in the movie, and a second one for *A Touch of Class* in 1973. She is now an MP, representing the Labour party.

It certainly seems, whether a raunchy movie is a great success or a big failure, it is always newsworthy. Whoever was to be cast in the lead roles of the *Fifty Shades of Grey* movie would become a world famous star. Before the cast could be announced, however, the studio and E.L. James had to agree on a director, someone who could turn the steamy novel into a movie that would be suitably raunchy but not so explicit that it would be off-putting to a potential audience.

In early 2013, it seemed new directors were being suggested every week by newspapers eager to reveal any *Fifty Shades* news. First, *Atonement* director Joe Wright was suggested for the job but his busy schedule didn't allow him to accept the role. *Good Will Hunting*'s Gus Van Sant reportedly filmed test scenes with actor Alex Pettyfer in a bid to win the job, and other directors in the mix, as reported by *Variety*, included *Monster*'s Patty Jenkins, *Dreamgirls*' Bill Condon and Steven Soderbergh, whose first movie was the provocative *Sex, Lies, and Videotape*.

On 19 June 2013 E.L. James announced via Twitter that a director had been hired: 'I'm delighted & thrilled to let you guys know that Sam Taylor-Johnson has agreed to direct the film of *Fifty Shades of Grey*.'

Croydon-born Sam Taylor-Johnson, formerly known as Sam Taylor-Wood, began her career as an artist, producing photography and video work that led to her being nominated for the prestigious Turner Prize in 1998. Previously married to art dealer Jay Jopling (they have two daughters), Sam began a relationship with actor Aaron Johnson in 2009, and the pair married in 2012, combining their surnames so they are now known as Sam and Aaron Taylor-Johnson. The couple, who have two daughters together, met when Sam directed Aaron in her first movie, the John Lennon biopic *Nowhere Boy*. Since she had not directed any other feature films following this debut, her appointment as director of the big budget, highly anticipated *Fifty Shades of Grey* movie did raise more than a few eyebrows.

'I am excited to be charged with the evolution of *Fifty Shades of Grey* from page to screen,' Taylor-Johnson said in an interview the day after her hiring was announced. 'For the legions of fans, I want to say that I will honour the power of Erika's book and the characters of Christian and Anastasia. They are under my skin too.'

Her producer, Michael De Luca, backed up the choice of Sam for the directing role, mentioning her 'unique ability to gracefully showcase complex relationships dealing with love, emotion and sexual chemistry.

'E.L. James's characters and vivid storytelling require a director who is willing to take risks and push the envelope where needed and Sam is a natural fit,' he added.

Insiders muttered that perhaps Taylor-Johnson was chosen because she was not that experienced – giving James and the producers more control over how the movie turned out – but it is more likely some of her previous work helped win her the job, including her contribution to *Destricted*, a compilation of short erotic films from 2006 that is now sold on DVD with a warning about the explicit scenes featured.

With a director now in place, and filming scheduled to start in late 2013, it was time for Sam Taylor-Johnson, the producers and E.L. James to choose a cast. The most important roles were, of course, the two leads, Anastasia Steele and Christian Grey, and the internet went into overdrive as fans of the novels speculated which actress and actor would – and should – win the parts.

Throughout the history of Hollywood, fans have always had an interest in who would bring their favourite fictional characters to life. Back in the 1930s, the casting of the two leads in the film adaptation of Margaret Mitchell's bestseller *Gone with the Wind* caused filming to be delayed by two years. Producer David O. Selznick wanted Clark Gable for the role of Rhett Butler, but he was under contract to another studio and a deal was eventually struck so he could appear in the movie, while a nationwide 'search for Scarlett' led to 1,400 actresses (including Katharine Hepburn, Joan Crawford, Norma Shearer and Tallulah Bankhead) being interviewed for the part of Scarlett O'Hara before Vivien Leigh was chosen.

And even if the producer and director have found their leading man or lady, it doesn't mean the fans are going to like it. James Bond fans were horrified that blond Daniel Craig was cast as the previously dark-haired 007 in 2005, with the *Daily Mirror* announcing his casting with the headline 'The Name's Bland – James Bland', while lovers of *Bridget Jones's Diary* were less than impressed when their favourite overweight British singleton was to be played by super-slim American actress Renée Zellweger.

Tom Cruise, meanwhile, has enraged fans of novels more than once, first when he was cast as blond, sexy and six-foot-tall vampire Lestat in the movie *Interview with the Vampire*. Not only were fans upset, but the novel's author, Anne Rice, was pretty unimpressed, too, and she went so far as to place an advert in industry newspaper *Variety* condemning his casting (she changed her mind after seeing the finished movie, saying 'That Tom did make Lestat work was something I could not see in a crystal ball. It's to his credit that he proved me wrong.') Tom did it again with Jack Reacher, based on Lee Child's series of thriller novels – the titular character is supposed to be tough, aggressive . . . and 6' 5" tall, blond, blue eyed and with a 50" chest. Although Child himself defended Cruise's casting ('With another actor you might get 100% of the height but only 90% of Reacher. With Tom you get 100% of Reacher with

90% of the height'), the film remains one of the lowest-grossing Tom Cruise movies in a decade.

While Taylor-Johnson, James and the producers were weighing up their options, they no doubt also considered the case of *Twilight*. By autumn 2007, the first three instalments of Stephenie Meyer's *Twilight* saga had been published and become a sensation – when the third book, *Eclipse*, came out in August 2007 it sold more than 150,000 copies in its first 24 hours on sale. When it was announced that a movie would be made of the first *Twilight* book, fans of the novels obsessed over who should be cast as the lovers Bella and her vampire Edward. And when Kristen Stewart was cast as Bella, Meyer was bombarded with hate messages and had to post a comment on her website stating that it wasn't her decision to make (she did not have casting approval) but she was happy with it – and fans should stop begging her to choose a good Edward as she had no control over casting.

On 11 December 2007, it was announced that Robert Pattinson had won the role and *Twilight* websites crashed as fans wrote about their disgust at the decision. 'I hate Robert!!! Edward is supposed to be hot and I think he's not . . . I don't like him!!!!!' 'THEY PICKED THE WRONG PERSON FOR EDWARD!!!!!!!!!!!!!!!!!!' and 'No offence or anything, but Robert Pattinson isn't good looking enough to be Edward,' were just some of the comments sent into the Twilight Lexicon fan-website while comments on Snarkerati.com included: 'Robert is not even remotely close to the Edward I imagined', 'I'm hoping there will be some freak accident and they'll have to change him' and 'He looks like a bum to me. Edward needs to be hot, they should recast or they're going to have a lot of disappointed fans.'

Of course, once the hugely successful movie was released, fans had changed their minds and Pattinson has since been voted Sexiest Man Alive two years in a row by *People* magazine and was one of *Glamour* magazine's Richest UK Actors Under 30, having earned an estimated £40 million last year. Oh, and the *Twilight* series of films has made over $3.3 billion worldwide.

Still, fans' fervour about their favourite characters can give a movie bad press even before a frame of film has been shot. Everyone involved in the production of *Fifty Shades of Grey* knew it was extremely important to get the casting of Christian Grey and Anastasia Steele just right, so that fans of the books would be happy, and E.L. James' characters would appear on screen just as she imagined them.

As far back as the summer of 2012, E.L. James had been asked whom she wanted in the roles of Christian and Ana. In an interview with RedCarpetNewsTV.com, James was asked, since *Twilight* had been an inspiration for *Fifty Shades*, whether Robert Pattinson and Kristen Stewart should take the roles. 'I think it would be too strange!' she laughed. 'It would just be . . . ugh . . . weird.' When pressed as to whether she had any actors in mind, James replied: 'I have about four people in mind for Ana and three for Christian but I'm not telling anyone what they are because I'm not allowed to discuss the movie at all, which is a real shame.'

James was also receiving fan suggestions via her Facebook page. 'On Facebook I've had a list of names as long as my arm. People have suggested Pierce Brosnan needs to play Christian!'

A British professor, Dr Faye Skelton from the University of Central Lancashire, even came up with a scientific photo composite to create a mug shot of what Christian should look like, based on the male celebrities that female fans of the novel had suggested for the role. The resulting photo featured hair from Channing Tatum and Brad Pitt, eyes from Patrick Dempsey and Johnny Depp, Chris Hemsworth's nose, David Beckham and Brad Pitt's jawlines and, rather surprisingly, Val Kilmer's lips. Dr Skelton told the *Daily Mail* that she used British police software to create every woman's dream Christian Grey. 'While we don't want to intrude on anyone's fantasies, based on a small sample of women, this is the image of Christian Grey they have in their heads when reading the novels. Personally, I think he's quite handsome!'

Certainly, if Dr Skelton's mug shot was anything to go by, fans had very strong opinions on just how Chrisitan should look. Soon the internet was buzzing with the names of actors supposedly in the running – or even secretly auditioning – for the role of Christian, and fans were weighing in with who they liked and disliked. So who were some of the contenders?

Ian Somerhalder

Thirty-six-year-old Somerhalder, a former model, is best known for two starring TV roles – as Boone, one of the survivors of the Oceanic Airlines crash in acclaimed series *Lost*, and more recently as the dark, sexy and lethal vampire Damon Salvatore in *The Vampire Diaries*. Somerhalder's name was often suggested by fans as a favourite for the role of Christian Grey (he has a huge teenage following, and girls who love him refer to him as 'Smolderholder'), but in interviews he revealed he would have been unable to accept the role as filming would have clashed with his ongoing work on *The Vampire Diaries*.

Chace Crawford

Texas-born Crawford made his film debut at the age of 20 in the film *The Covenant*, but he will always be remembered for his role as rich boy Nate Archibald in the TV series *Gossip Girl*, that ran from 2007 to 2012. One of the stars of the comedy movie *What to Except When You're Expecting*, Chace was briefly tipped to play Christian, but instead accepted a role in the movie *Undrafted*, and made an appearance in two episodes of the series *Glee*.

Ryan Gosling

Gosling – one of the hottest actors in Hollywood – famously began his career at the age of 12 as a member of Disney's Mickey Mouse Club (alongside future stars such as Britney Spears and Justin Timberlake). It was starring roles as an adult in movies such as *Murder by Numbers* and *The Believer* that got him noticed in Hollywood, and he became the name on many a woman's lips after he played the romantic lead in *The Notebook* in 2004 when he was 24. By 2010 he was winning acclaim for roles in movies such as *Blue Valentine*, and he went on to make *Crazy Stupid Love*, *Drive*, *The Ides of March* and *The Place Beyond the Pines*. Gosling was reportedly approached to play the role of Christian – and his legion of female fans would have rejoiced – but apparently he turned the part down.

Stephen Amell

The star of television's *Arrow*, Canadian actor Stephen Amell publicly stated he didn't want the role of Christian Grey, despite fans calling for his casting. 'I didn't find his character to be totally redeeming,' he told TV show *Access Hollywood*. 'I actually didn't find him to be that interesting . . . Nothing about Christian Grey really spoke to me.'

Matt Bomer

'Matt who?' you ask. While most people haven't heard of Matt Bomer, he nonetheless became the focus of a dedicated internet fan campaign to be cast in the role of Christian. The 37-year-old Texan actor began his career in daytime US soaps, appearing in *All My Children* and then *Guiding Light*, before earning small roles in movies like *In Time* and *Magic Mike*. By late 2012, internet polls had him leading the race to win the part of Christian – in fans' eyes, at least. After Bomer publicly announced he was gay in 2012, author Bret Easton Ellis (yes, him again) tweeted that '*Fifty Shades of Grey* demands an actor that is genuinely into women' and 'Matt Bomer isn't right for Christian Grey because he is openly gay. He's great for other roles but this is too big a game', but numerous fans rose to Bomer's defence, including one of his co-stars, Willie Garson, who played Carrie's gay pal Stanford on *Sex and The City* for years. 'People assumed I was gay, but it's acting, I'm not gay. When I was on *NYPD Blue*, nobody asked me if I was a murderer.' He added in a Press Association interview that 'the Matt thing with the Christian Grey thing has just gotten so ridiculous,' adding that fans' internet campaigns to win Matt the role were 'insane, it is actually insane,' as neither fans or the media had any say in the casting.

There was just as much speculation about who would play Ana. Actresses supposedly in the mix included Elizabeth Olsen, who had won praise for her role in *Martha Marcy May Marlene*; Shailene Woodley, best known as George Clooney's daughter in *The Descendants* and for her superb performance as a teen dying of cancer in *The Fault in Our Stars*; British actress Felicity Jones and Swedish actress Alicia Vikander.

On 2 September 2013, however, the announcement came. 'I am delighted to let you know that the lovely Dakota Johnson has agreed to be our Anastasia in the film adaptation of *Fifty Shades of Grey*,' tweeted E.L. James, and then a few minutes later she sent another tweet. 'The gorgeous and talented Charlie Hunnam will be Christian Grey in the film adaptation of *Fifty Shades of Grey*.'

It was a surprise, as just two weeks earlier in an interview, representatives for actor Charlie Hunnam had denied he was going to star in the movie. Two days after the official announcement of his casting, there was already a huge backlash over the news. Thousands of fans took to the campaigning web platform Change.org to object to the casting, and campaign for Matt Bomer and TV actress Alexis Bledel to be given the roles. 'Matt Bomer is the perfect description of Christian and Alexis Bledel is the perfect actress to represent Anastasia and if they are not, nobody will be,' wrote one of 17,000 people who signed the petition.

While there was some fan annoyance about the casting of unknown Dakota Johnson – many fans wanted Alexis Bledel, best known for her lead role in TV's *Gilmore Girls* – it was Hunnam's casting as Christian that caused the most online ire. He's a British actor known for his muscles and sex appeal, so it was hard to see why some die-hard *Fifty Shades* fans were so against him. Born in Newcastle in 1980, Hunnam became an actor after being expelled from secondary school (he completed his exams at home) and then attending the Cumbria College of Art and Design where he studied film. Discovered by a production manager in a shoe shop when he was playing around with his brother, he was cast in the children's TV series *Byker Grove*. By the age of 18 he had won his first major role, as schoolboy Nathan in the gay comedy drama *Queer as Folk*, before relocating to Los Angeles and appearing in movies such as *Cold Mountain*, *Nicholas Nickleby* and *Children of Men*.

It was his role in the gritty US television series *Sons of Anarchy* that turned Charlie into a pin-up in 2008. Following an outlaw motorcycle club in California of which his character, Jax, was the vice president, the rough, tough series made him a TV star – but fans of *Fifty Shades* probably weren't so keen on his onscreen persona: long and lank haired, unshaven, clad in jeans and a biker jacket – not exactly the polished image they expected for suave millionaire businessman Christian Grey.

One of the film's producers, Dana Brunetti, turned to Twitter to defend the choice of Charlie. 'There is a lot that goes into casting that isn't just looks. Talent, availability, their desire to do it, chemistry with other actors, etc,' he wrote. 'So if your favourite wasn't cast, then it is most likely due to something on that list. Keep that in mind while hating and keep perspective.'

When asked about his controversial casting, Charlie Hunnam took it in his stride, addressing rumours that he had turned the role down once, before later accepting it. 'I met with Sam Taylor-Johnson a couple of times,' he told a press conference. 'We talked at length about the role, the movie and what her intention was. I felt really intrigued and excited about it so I went and read the first book to get a clearer idea of who this character was, and I felt even more excited at the prospect of bringing him to life.' He even chatted about the sex scenes that would no doubt be in the movie. 'You know what, I had such a baptism of fire with regards to sexuality on camera at the beginning of my career,' he told the Associated Press, talking about the UK series *Queer as Folk*. 'There were some incredible, explicit sex scenes on that show with a man. Now I am 16 years older and more mature, so I don't anticipate them being too much of a problem. It's like anything else, just an exciting challenge.'

Hunnam made that statement in September 2013, but just a few weeks later, on 12 October, a shock announcement was made: Charlie Hunnam would no longer be starring in *Fifty Shades of Grey*. Universal Pictures issued a press release saying: 'The filmmakers of *Fifty Shades of Grey* and Charlie Hunnam have agreed to find another male lead given Hunnam's immersive TV schedule [on *Sons of Anarchy*] which is not allowing him time to adequately prepare for the role of Christian Grey.'

Soon Hollywood was buzzing with the news. According to industry paper the *Hollywood Reporter*, Charlie Hunnam – who is also a writer – had submitted his own notes on the script, and while these were well received, when he asked for more script approval he wasn't given it. The *Hollywood Reporter* also noted that another source hinted that Charlie had butted heads with various people, including the director, and rumours circled that all was not well on set. On the day that Universal hired writer Patrick Marber to polish the script, Charlie Hunnam decided that – even though he would be walking away from a rumoured $125,000 salary and would burn bridges with a major movie studio in the process – it was time to leave the project.

Producer Michael De Luca was quick to deny reports that fan reaction was the reason Hunnam no longer had the part. 'I am on Twitter constantly, I am a masochist,' he told reporters at the *Hollywood Reporter*'s Producers Round-table discussion in November. He was aware that Hunnam 'wasn't what most readers pictured' as Christian Grey but stated that 'we're not making the movie based on Twitter.' He also reiterated the official reason that Charlie Hunnam had walked away from the role. 'In terms of schedule, to be free from *Sons of Anarchy* in time to show up on the set of our movie, the physical transformation and the psychological transformation from Jax (Hunnam's TV character) to Christian Grey was more than he could accomplish in the time we had.'

Meanwhile, E.L. James told *Entertainment Weekly* magazine that Charlie's exit was 'disappointing, but it is what it is. I wish him well.'

It was only eight months later, in June 2014, that Hunnam finally spoke about his decision. 'I felt like I had an interesting take on that character and felt like I could have done a good job of playing Christian Grey, otherwise I wouldn't have taken it on in the first place,' he told *Life & Style*. 'When you put the time into something like that and a character comes alive in your mind, it's heartbreaking not to be able to play him. It was definitely kind of heartbreaking having to say goodbye to that character and not bring it to life.'

When asked whether he'd see the movie with his replacement in the role of Christian, Charlie added: 'If they invite me to the premiere, I will go and see it there. If not, I'll go and buy some tickets on opening night.' (Later that month, he claimed that he had seen a lengthy clip of the still-to-be-completed film and he 'loved it'.)

It wasn't the first time an actor had walked away or been relieved of a leading role in a movie, but it was certainly one of the most high-profile examples. In the past, probably the best-known recasting decisions had been on *Back to the Future* – Michael J. Fox replaced Eric Stoltz in the lead role even though Stoltz had already filmed some scenes – and on *The Lord of the Rings* trilogy where Stuart Townsend had started off in the role of Aragorn, only to be replaced by Viggo Mortensen. But both of these instances were in an age before every tidbit of news was splashed over the internet, so the frenzy that followed Hunnam's decision to pull out was unique.

It certainly gave websites a good excuse to speculate about who would become Christian Grey (again) and also to run lots of photos of good-looking actors who were potentially in the running. Matt Bomer's name was put forward once again, and was joined by *The Borgias'* actor François Arnaud, Clint Eastwood's son Scott Eastwood, *True Blood* star Alexander Skarsgård . . . and a young Irish actor named Jamie Dornan.

Eleven days after the news that Charlie Hunnam had quit the production, Universal Pictures announced to *Variety* that Jamie Dornan had been hired and would be taking on the role of Christian Grey. *Variety* revealed that Jamie and actor Billy Magnussen – a stage actor also known for his role in daytime soap *As the World Turns* – had been asked to record a screen test the previous week, and the decision had been made shortly afterwards.

Jamie had flown back to the UK from Los Angeles shortly after the audition and had to wait by the phone to find out whether the part was his. As he told *Entertainment Weekly* magazine, at 1.30 a.m. (5.30 p.m. in Los Angeles), I was sort of pretending I wasn't waiting, but the phone was in my hand, halfway to my ear.' It finally rang, and when he answered, it was director Sam Taylor-Johnson on the other end, telling him that he was, indeed, Christian Grey. 'There was a slight fear,' he added, about getting the news, 'but beyond anything else, I was really f**king excited.'

As he told *EW*'s reporter Nicole Sperling, the subject matter of the book hadn't deterred him from accepting the role. 'I'm a fairly worldly guy. I grew up in a very liberal place. I'm not saying we had a playroom, but I'm not perturbed or shocked by [the sex in the book]. It's essential to the story. I can't believe films that don't invoke the sexual side of it. So it works for me.'

In his interview with *EW*, Jamie revealed he had actually sent producers an audition tape during the first round of casting, but he wasn't asked to do a screen test until Hunnam dropped out. Of course, within days of his hiring, Jamie realised the daunting nature of what he had taken on, as paparazzi camped outside his home and fans took to the internet to applaud or boo his casting. In the *Entertainment Weekly* interview, he acknowledged that there were many fans of the book who cared about how it would be turned into a film, and especially how their beloved character Christian Grey would be portrayed. He realised that not everyone was pleased with his casting, but promised that he would do his best to bring Christian to life on the screen.

E.L. James, at least, was certainly pleased with his casting. Following the mixed reaction to Charlie Hunnam's brief flirtation with the role, she had commented that 'I had to get off Twitter for a couple of days [due to the fan reaction].' But when Jamie was announced, she told *Entertainment Weekly*, the fan response was 'so positive'. 'It was so lovely that people didn't know who he was,' she added. 'I loved that.'

Fans were actually already much happier with the choice of Jamie. *Girls* creator and star Lena Dunham tweeted her pleasure: 'I'm a monstrous fan. Wasn't allowed to be attracted to him on *The Fall* bc he played a sexmurderer. 50 Shades is my big chance.'

One of Jamie's own friends wasn't so keen. 'A friend of mine texted me saying "I heard about *Fifty Shades*. Congratulations on the role. That's going to be disgusting. I won't watch it."'

Charlie Hunnam, meanwhile, offered encouragement to the actor who had replaced him. 'I'm sure he'll do a great job,' he told TMZ in November 2013. 'I don't really know his work but I know Sam [Taylor-Johnson], the director, is amazing, and she has fantastic taste, so I'm sure he'll do a great job.'

Of course, all the fuss about the Charlie-to-Jamie cast change caused problems with the shooting schedule of the movie. When Hunnam had been announced in the lead role, shooting was due to begin in Vancouver, Canada, on 5 November,

2013, and the film's release date was scheduled for 1 August, 2014. Following the cast change, shooting was rescheduled to begin on 1 December 2013, with producer Dana Brunetti announcing the first day of filming by tweeting a photo of the film slate from the set that afternoon, with the caption 'Here we go.' The release date of the movie was also changed from summer 2014 to Valentine's Day (14 February) 2015. *Entertainment Weekly* magazine speculated that the new release date was much better, as when the film had been scheduled to open in August 2014, it would have been sharing cinemas with blockbusters such as the comic book *Guardians of the Galaxy* (that went on to be the biggest box office smash of 2014), a new Transformers movie and a Planet of the Apes sequel, whereas in February 2015 it would be released at a less crowded time.

'Together with the international marketing and distribution team, we've been looking really closely at the August date and becoming more and more convinced that the right thing to do for the movie was to push it,' Universal Pictures chairman Donna Langley commented. 'So even if Charlie had stayed, we still would have been making the date change.'

Plans were set in motion for filming to begin, with production magazine *Production Weekly* revealing that the movie's working title (used to book studios, rent equipment and hire crew without revealing what movie they are working on) was to be 'The Adventures of Max and Banks', and that casting calls were being posted for lucky extras in Los Angeles and Vancouver.

With shooting to start just a couple of weeks after the announcement of Jamie's casting, the actor didn't have much time to prepare for the role – though one thing he did have to try before filming began was dancing, for a scene in which his character would glide effortlessly across the dance floor. Usually this wouldn't be too daunting for an actor, but – as Jamie revealed in an interview with TV presenter Graham Norton – he couldn't even walk properly!

Apparently, people had always commented on the way Jamie walked and he was very aware that he walked differently from everyone else. 'I have quite pronounced calf muscles and my mate once said to me: "Do you know why you have big calves?" I said I thought it was because my dad does, it's hereditary, but my mate said "No, it's because you walk on your tiptoes!" I was first really conscious of it on the first day on set for *The Fall* – the producer said I should take longer strides. Because I am on my tiptoes I am quite high and bouncy so my wife suggested I try leaning back when I walk which looked even worse. Then I learned I had to dance for *Fifty Shades*. I can't dance at all, so I had dance lessons and the teacher's suggestion when I was really struggling was – 'You should just think of it as walking!'. . . The wrong thing to say! He explained I should just go heel to toe, heel to toe, so now I do that every day and I can walk!'

In between dance lessons, there was little time to get ready for the attention the media spotlight immediately thrust upon him as he arrived with pregnant wife Amelia in Canada. With sets in Vancouver being prepared and casting of the supporting characters being finalised, Jamie and his co-star, Dakota Johnson, posed for a series of photos for *Entertainment Weekly* magazine, appearing in the kind of clothes Christian Grey and Anastasia Steele would be seen wearing in the movie

– including, on the cover of the magazine, a photo of Jamie holding the silk tie fans of the book remember well.

In the accompanying interview, Jamie talked about the pressure of being cast as Christian, and not being afraid of the sexuality that would be a big part of the movie. Since he had already met his co-star Dakota and director Sam when he auditioned, Jamie had an idea of what the experience would be like when he accepted the role.

One thing some actors would be worried about was appearing nude, or at least semi-clothed, for the camera, but this didn't faze Jamie either (no surprise when you remember he used to model Calvin Klein underpants). 'I take decent enough care of myself anyway,' Jamie commented about the upcoming nude scenes, 'so obviously I'm gonna up it slightly with training, but we don't have any intention to really bulk up. I don't think it's appropriate.'

He wasn't the only one in the movie who would be baring some flesh, however. Little known actress Dakota Johnson would be in the scenes with him, and at just 24 years old, had less experience in front of the camera, clothes on or off. She wasn't completely naïve, however, as Johnson had spent most of her life on movie sets, accompanying her famous parents – Don Johnson and Melanie Griffith.

Born in Austin, Texas on 4 October 1989, Dakota is actually a third-generation Hollywood star – her grandmother (Melanie's mother) is Tippi Hedren, best known for being Alfred Hitchcock's muse in the movie *The Birds*. Raised in Aspen, Colorado, Dakota actually began her career not as an actress like her famous relatives, but as a model. 'The whole thing really started when I was 12, when I did a *Teen Vogue* shoot with celebrity kids,' she told *Aspen Peak* magazine. 'It was fun for me. I didn't do anything more for a few years after that, then I signed with IMG [model agency]. When I turned 18 it all started coming together.'

Dakota's home life, meanwhile, was somewhat complicated. Mum Melanie and dad Don Johnson had met on a film set, when he was 22 and she was the 14-year-old daughter of his co-star, Tippi Hedren. 'She fell almost instantly in love with him,' Hedren told *People* magazine. 'It was an adolescent crush.' The couple began living together when Melanie was just 15, got engaged when she was 18, and married months later at a chapel in Las Vegas. The marriage lasted less than a year. 'It just wasn't working for us, but we couldn't split up,' Melanie told *People* years later. 'We thought it might work better if we were married. It didn't. I got married in order to end the relationship.'

After the split, Melanie found her career in Hollywood rising, while Johnson won the lead role of Sonny Crockett in the hit TV series *Miami Vice*. But despite short-lived marriages to other people, the pair worked better together than apart and reunited after Johnson offered Melanie a guest-star role in his show. By early 1989 they were back together and announced that Melanie was pregnant with Don's daughter – Dakota. The couple stayed together until 1994, when they separated then reconciled, and then they split permanently in 1995.

Later that year, Melanie began a relationship with her co-star on the film *Two Much*, Spanish actor Antonio Banderas. Once her divorce was finalised from Don, Banderas and Melanie married in May 1996, when Dakota was seven. She soon had a long list of siblings to add to her celebrity family – Melanie and Antonio had a daughter, Stella, in 1996, while Johnson has had three children with wife Kelley Phleger. And Dakota has more siblings from her parents' previous marriages, too – older half-brother Alexander (from her mother's marriage to actor Steven Bauer), and older half-brother Jesse (from her dad's relationship with Patti D'Arbanville).

Dividing her time between her parents, Dakota was often on set with them and actually made her own movie debut at the age of ten, starring with her half-sister Stella Banderas in *Crazy in Alabama*. The girls played the daughters of their real-life mother Melanie, while Dakota's stepdad Antonio directed. The film wasn't a success, but it did give Dakota a taste of life in front of the camera, and by the time she was a teenager she had decided to model while training to be an actress. Back in 2009, she told *Aspen Peak* magazine: 'Everyone has that thing that sparks some sort of emotion in them. Acting does that for me. It's about learning and storytelling. I don't know where I am going to be tomorrow or in a week. I don't know what's going to happen, and I'm not rushing anywhere. I know I'll be working with IMG [Model Agency] . . . but I know I'm going to be an actress.'

In 2006, Dakota was voted Miss Golden Globe, an honour bestowed on the daughter (or occasionally, son) of a celebrity, who assists in presenting at the Golden Globe Awards. A prestigious honour for the children of actors and actresses – Laura Dern (daughter of Bruce Dern and Diane Ladd), Bruce Willis' daughter Rumer and Clint Eastwood's daughters Kathryn and Francesca have all won the job – it was especially rewarding for

Dakota, as she was the first daughter of a Miss Golden Globe (Melanie won in 1975) who had been given the honour. 'It was terrifying,' she told WENN News at the time. 'You bring the Golden Globes out and you give them to the very talented people . . . I was 16 and I was terrified. I was wearing these gloves and I kept thinking that they were gonna slip out of my hands. I was gonna be the girl that dropped a Golden Globe on the stage and, like, ruin everything. I don't even remember the night, honestly, I was so terrified!'

When she graduated from high school two years later, Dakota signed with the William Morris acting agency and started out on her career. For her first role in 2010, she co-starred as Amelia Ritter in the Facebook movie *The Social Network*, alongside Jesse Eisenberg, Justin Timberlake and Andrew Garfield, and followed it with a part in the teen drama *Beastly*. Other small roles in movies like *21 Jump Street* and *The Five Year Engagement* followed, and in March 2012 it was announced that Dakota would star as Kate in the new TV comedy series *Ben and Kate*, alongside Nat Faxon. While the show only lasted one season, it brought Dakota to the attention of Hollywood producers who cast her in the action movie *Need for Speed*, and in the lead role of Imogen in a new adaptation of Shakespeare's *Cymbeline*.

It was, however, the announcement in September 2013, that Dakota had been chosen to play Anastasia Steele, that got everybody talking. Who was this young woman who had won one of the most coveted roles in Hollywood, and how did she feel about baring all for the role?

In the *Entertainment Weekly* interview that introduced Jamie and Dakota to the world, she commented: 'Obviously I want to look good naked,' and on working out for the first time in her life for the role: 'I totally understand now why people exercise, because you kind of fucking feel awesome!'

The magazine added that Dakota had campaigned hard for the role of Anastasia, and had acted in numerous auditions with different actors who were potential Christian Greys. She was obviously well aware of what the role entailed, to the point that she admitted she wouldn't let her parents anywhere near the set, or to the premiere either, as she didn't think it was appropriate for them to see their daughter so exposed on screen.

Indeed, in an interview with Indiewire, Melanie Griffith admitted she knew Dakota wouldn't want her to see the movie. 'She was like, "You guys cannot come. There's no way." So we're not going!'

Certainly, both Dakota's parents – and her stepdad – could give her advice about explicit performances in movies and how to handle them. Don Johnson starred in the controversial sexual drama *The Harrad Experiment* and equally explicit *A Boy and His Dog* early on in his career, while Melanie Griffith played a young nymphomaniac in one of her first screen roles (in *The Drowning Pool*) and followed it with a leading role as porn actress in the sexual drama *Body Double*. Stepdad Antonio Banderas, meanwhile, is no stranger to raunchy roles either, having made movies for Spanish director Pedro Almodóvar early on in his career, including *Law of Desire*, *Matador* and *Tie Me Up! Tie Me Down!*. When she was asked at a *Vanity Fair* party, however, mum Melanie said she would only be there when her daughter needed her. 'It's her movie, you know what I mean? It'd be weird if mom and dad were there and Antonio and all of the family. It would just be awkward. But I'm sure it will be great. I really love Sam [Taylor-Johnson]. And Dakota has a really good head on her shoulders. She's no dummy.'

There was certainly a lot of pressure on both Dakota and Jamie when it came to the raunchier aspects of the movie. As it went into production on 1 December, producer Dana Brunetti talked about the explicit nature of *Fifty Shades*: 'What we're kind of hearing from the fans is they want it dirty . . . they want it as close as possible [to the book]'. The worry for the producers was that if the film went in to as much detail as the novel, it may receive the dreaded NC-17 rating in the US, which often hampers box office takings as some cinema chains refuse to show NC-17 movies. 'I always thought it would be really cool if we released the R version [similar to Britain's 18 certificate] and then we had an NC-17 version that we released a few weeks later,' he explained. 'Everybody could go and enjoy the R version, and then if they really wanted to see it again and get a little bit more gritty with it, then have that NC-17 version out there as well.'

Brunetti told Collider.com that he did not 'want this film to be seen as mommy porn – we want to keep it elevated but also give the fans what they want.'

What fans wanted straight away were pictures of Jamie and Dakota on set and in action as Christian and Anastasia, and they weren't disappointed. As filming kicked off in December 2013 in the Gastown district of Vancouver, Canada, media photographers were there to catch glimpses of the two actors in character for the first time. On the first day of filming, Jamie and Dakota were spotted filming a scene in which Christian and Ana were chatting over coffee – Jamie in a smart grey suit and Dakota, with dyed brown hair (she's naturally blonde), in a casual green jacket and scarf as the less sophisticated Ana.

As Vancouver residents began keeping an eye out to see where the *Fifty Shades* crew would be filming next, the production team announced who else would be joining the cast of the most eagerly anticipated movie of 2015. TV actress Eloise Mumford was to be Ana's roommate Kate, *True Blood*'s Luke Grimes accepted the role of Christian's adopted brother Elliot Grey, British singer Rita Ora was cast as Christian's sister Mia, and acclaimed actresses Jennifer Ehle (best known for her role in *Pride and Prejudice*) and Marcia Gay Harden (who won an Oscar for her role in *Pollock*) won the roles of Ana's mother Carla and Christian's mother Grace, respectively. *Pacific Rim*'s Max Martini would play Christian's bodyguard Taylor, *24*'s Callum Keith Rennie was to be Ana's stepdad Ray, Scottish actor Andrew Airlie was cast as Christian's dad, and *Dawson's Creek*'s Dylan Neal as Bob, Carla's current husband.

All of the cast and crew had just three months to bring the characters and stories of *Fifty Shades* to life, with filming scheduled to run from 1 December 2013 until 21 February 2014. Some of the shoot was difficult, due to some especially cold and snowy Vancouver weather – a bicycle scene due to be filmed in Gastown had to be cancelled due to the snow on one day in December.

Vancouver landmarks were used to create some of the places in Seattle where Christian and Ana meet in the book – the striking glass restaurant the Bentall V Cactus Club Café doubled as the entrance to Grey Enterprises, with the crew unloading hundreds of trees at the entrance to make it appear as if it were spring although they were filming in deepest winter, while the tower itself – Bentall V Tower – became Christian's imposing office building. The University of British Columbia doubled as Washington State University (where Christian makes a speech at Ana's graduation), while the Vancouver Fairmont Hotel became the Heathman Hotel, where Christian keeps a room.

Nicknamed 'Hollywood North', Vancouver has long been a popular filming location for American movie makers tired of using the same US locations that have been seen a million times before. As well as *Fifty Shades*, movies such as the four *Twilight* films, the 2014 *Godzilla* remake and the 2015 Disney movie George Clooney-starring *Tomorrowland*, were all filmed in the city, as were episodes of *The X-Files*, *Fringe* and the fantasy show Jamie himself had co-starred in, *Once Upon a Time*.

No production had as many eyes on it as the *Fifty Shades of Grey* film, however. TV news camera crews hovered around Vancouver to capture anything they could, and reports appeared in the press about how filming was going – and not all the rumours were good. While producer Michael De Luca commented that the chemistry between the two leads was 'hot' and 'the chemistry is there, they genuinely like each other', there was news that not everyone was happy on set. Gossip magazines reported there was tension between director Sam Taylor-Johnson and writer E.L. James, with a source telling E! News: 'Sam is getting annoyed about the way the script is being handled. E.L. James wants the movie to match the book exactly, but Sam has a different perspective. Sam is reminding E.L. she writes books, and [Sam] makes movies. This has caused some tension between the two of them.'

The same unnamed source did say some things were going well on set. 'Jamie is really protective over Dakota. She is very friendly and talks to everyone, Jamie stays to himself and doesn't talk much. Jamie thinks Dakota gets really distracted, because she is so nice to people and so he will walk over to who she is talking to and try and end the conversation. He is nice about it, but he does ask them to leave her alone.'

E! News's source also added that everyone on set loved Dakota, and that everything was going well thanks to the friendly relationships between cast and crew. 'Sam has a great relationship with the actors. The script is running smoothly, and there is not a lot of reshooting that has had to be done.'

The talk of tension between author and director didn't go away, however, until E.L. James poked fun at the rumours when she posted a photo on Twitter of her and Sam showing off their best fight poses with the caption 'The gloves are off!'

Despite the media reports of friction, it seemed like the set was generally a fun place to be, with E.L. James posting photos of her on Charlie Tango, Christian's helicopter in the movie, and Rita Ora revealing in an interview before the Grammy Awards that the movie would contain 'the biggest and most amazing shock ever', whipping fans into a frenzy, wondering what on earth she meant. (Ora also revealed that she had a little help on the set of her first movie – she wore an earpiece with someone feeding her her lines off camera as she couldn't remember them. 'I had to have someone in my ear on set telling me what to say before I said it because I was honestly like, so nervous, I forgot everything I had learnt,' she told *Access Hollywood*).

And Dakota's mum, Melanie Griffith, revealed she had seen

the one place fans really wanted to know about – Christian's infamous 'playroom' (described by Anastasia as his 'red room of pain' due to all the S&M paraphernalia). 'I did go visit for a couple of days when they were shooting just normal stuff,' Melanie told Indiewire. 'I did see the room of pain – I did go in there and check it out!'

Just days into production, there was something to take Jamie's mind off all the press speculation about his role as Christian and all the prying eyes wanting to get a look at the set. On 16 December 2013, it was announced that Jamie's wife Amelia had given birth to a baby girl – the biggest surprise being that she had given birth in Vancouver at the end of November, and no one had found out about it until a few weeks later – in fact, it was so secret that when the news got out, media reports got their facts wrong and stated Jamie and Amelia had had a baby boy.

It was straight back onto the set for Jamie, however, and as the year ended and 2014 began, the cast and crew continued filming and new information about the movie began to appear in the press and online. A website for Christian's business sprang up – www.greyenterprisesholdings.com – asking for people to submit interest for their internship program, and a huge billboard featuring Jamie's silhouette from behind, looking out over a Seattle skyline with the words 'Mr Grey Will See You Now' emblazoned across it became the first official announcement that the movie would open on Valentine's Day in 2015.

Fans were so desperate for any news from the shy Jamie that when he tweeted 'looking forward to 2015' (presumably referring to when *Fifty Shades* would be released) on 1 January

2014, his tweet was retweeted more than 5000 times. Those who hadn't known Jamie from his modelling days, his role in *The Fall* or *Once Upon a Time* wanted any information they could get about the man who would be Christian, though his co-star Marcia Gay Harden, who was playing the Mrs Grey (aka Christian's mum) thought the fact Jamie was relatively unknown was actually a good thing.

'I think the point is to have somebody mysterious because if you have somebody with too much pedigree to them . . . you can't stop thinking about the pedigree,' she said in an interview. 'I think that would be very hard to do for that role, so I think it's good that he's a bit of a mystery.'

When pressed, Marcia did add that Jamie was 'beautiful. He's chiselled beauty and the camera eats it up. He's an Irish boy . . . A UK-based actor who has done a bit of film. He just had a baby . . . he's a sweet guy. He does surfing. He sings little Irish ditties occasionally!'

Marcia was also asked whether, for her, making *Fifty Shades* with its racy tone was different from making other movies. 'If you are not in the red playroom of pain and pleasure with some naked flesh in your face and a sex toy in your hand, the experience of shooting the movie is much like doing any other movie,' she laughed.

Another co-star, singer turned actress Rita Ora (who plays Christian's sister Mia in the movie), also gushed about the film during an interview with Capital FM radio. 'The movie is amazing, it's such a great passionate movie,' she revealed. 'I had to be involved. I love the books. I know everybody's going to watch it, whether it's in secret or confidence, but everyone's going to watch it. It's going to be fun!'

Victor Rasuk, cast as the photographer, Jose, who is Anastasia's friend, also let a little information slip about the movie. 'I've been sworn to secrecy but I will say this: Dakota was amazing. Jamie was amazing. It was one of those things where we came into it wanting to do it justice. And I think all the fans, the millions of fans, will also love what we did. I think we did it justice.'

Unfortunately, not much more could be said, as Jamie confirmed a few weeks later in an interview with *Grazia* magazine in Italy. 'I cannot say anything about the movie!' he laughed. 'The production has imposed absolute silence.'

Director Sam Taylor-Johnson wouldn't be drawn on the movie either. At the premiere of *Godzilla*, starring her husband, Aaron Taylor-Johnson, she did admit she had sneaked him into the movie in a small role, while he commented: 'Hush, hush, don't give anything away yet,' with a secretive smile.

Occasionally, author E.L. James would reveal little snippets of the on-set action via her Twitter feed, exciting fans with snaps of Charlie Tango – Christian's helicopter – that she got to fly from the set in and tweeting a photo of the crew setting up for a shot at Boundary Bay Airport in which Christian takes Ana gliding. Most fun of all, perhaps, was her tweet when the cast and crew were filming at the store doubling for Claytons (the hardware store where Anastasia works) – of a pack of cable ties like the ones Christian buys (along with rope and masking tape), presumably for his S&M games.

The film's co-producer, Michael De Luca, did reveal how the crew were approaching adapting the novel for the screen. 'The movie can't be as explicit as the book,' he said at a breakfast for producers at the Sundance Film Festival. 'The book is explicit by design because the author wanted to go inside the head of Ana – the female lead – and detail her experience. On the literary level, that was necessary. But in a film or any visual medium, a picture is worth a thousand words. To be erotic on-screen is going to have more power than to read the words on a page.' He added that adapting the book was easier on him than it was for author E.L. James because 'we had to lose some stuff. We had to create some stuff.' And his inspiration was director Adrian Lyne, because his movies 'are classy and erotic without being exploitative'.

British director Adrian Lyne's movies are a good reference point for *Fifty Shades* – after all, this is the director who made one of the most famous erotic movies of all time, *9½ Weeks*. Lyne was also behind the camera for *Fatal Attraction, Indecent Proposal*, the remake of *Lolita* and *Unfaithful* – all movies known for their mix of drama and sex scenes. *9½ Weeks*, of course, had love scenes that made stars Mickey Rourke and Kim Basinger infamous (and forever associated with a fridge), while Michael Douglas and Glenn Close will always be associated with the erotic thriller *Fatal Attraction*, Demi Moore would score one of her biggest hits with the drama *Indecent Proposal*, and Richard Gere and Diane Lane would receive praise for their roles in the adultery movie *Unfaithful*. If De Luca and his team were using Lyne's movies as a guide for how to bring *Fifty Shades* to the screen, they were making a smart decision.

Fans, meanwhile, could only speculate as to what the movie would be like as filming wound down in Vancouver. On 21 February 2014, E.L. James tweeted 'And that's a wrap . . .' to confirm that filming had ended, and the following day, Jamie was spotted at the local airport, signing autographs while waiting for his flight back to London with his wife and new baby daughter. While most actors finishing a movie – and especially those with a new baby – would think about sitting back and relaxing for a few months, Jamie had just a couple of weeks at home before he would be heading off for work again, this time to revisit his most famous role so far.

In the meantime, speculation about *Fifty Shades* reached fever pitch. A teaser trailer was shown to the film industry in March 2014, presented by Universal Pictures' chairman Donna Langley at CinemaCon (an industry convention). 'Nobody outside the studio has seen a frame of footage,' she announced, before presenting a clip showing Dakota and Jamie meeting in Grey's office, at the hardware store where Ana works and at a coffee shop. Meanwhile, three months later on 18 June 2014, the first photo from the set of Jamie in character was released to the press. It showed Jamie, as Christian Grey, looking at the camera from behind the wheel of his Audi R8 and received a surprisingly mixed reaction from fans on the movie's Facebook page.

'That's NOT Christian! Yeah, I'll just stick to the books and keep him the way I want him . . .' wrote Sherry Costello, while another fan of the book, Ruta Dikgogodi Senoge added: 'Very much disappointed at the choice of actor to play Christian Grey. This is so not him!!! Super bad choice . . .' Others, however, disagreed. 'I AM DROOLING' tweeted @purple–witch while Stacey Heward described him as 'The perfect Christian Grey! Just how I imagined him to be. Perfect in everyway. Absolutely gorgeous.'

With more than six months to wait for the movie's release,

fans were chomping at the bit for any information, and even fell for an internet hoax that people thought was a risqué shot from the movie of Jamie standing over a blindfolded woman that was supposedly posted on his Instagram account. It turned out that Jamie didn't even have an Instagram account, and that the photo was actually from a *GQ* shoot he did with model Rosie Huntington-Whiteley!

Throughout, despite being followed by tabloid newspapers desperate to get a photo of him out and about with Amelia and their new baby, Jamie kept a low profile. Whereas other actors may have capitalised on their new-found fame by attending premieres and parties, Jamie returned to the quiet family life he had loved before the whole *Fifty Shades* madness had kicked off. In April 2014, Jamie's dad, Professor Jim Dornan, gave an interview with Northwest Prime radio in Seattle, where he was promoting his new book, *An Everyday Miracle*. While the interviewer mainly talked about Jim's area of expertise – pregnancy, birth and women's health – the conversation did touch on Jamie and his sudden huge fame.

'We are dealing with his fame in a grounded way, as he is,' said Jim. 'He is a very grounded young man and certainly nothing [like fame] goes to his head. He's a private man, understandably. We enjoy people thinking he's done a good job.'

Jim also talked about his family and how supported Jamie is in his newfound fame. 'His sisters are protective of him but it's nearly the other way round, they really look up to him too. We're a tight family and they all look to each other – and when you have lost your mum, like they did in their late teens, it does bind them close together and that bond will be there forever. And they are proud of him and love him.'

If Jamie and his family thought the interest in Jamie had reached fever pitch, they were mistaken. In June, Jamie appeared – in just his pants, in a bath – in photos for American magazine *Interview*, and talked about becoming Christian Grey onscreen. He admitted that more about Christian's character would be revealed than in the book, and that part of his personality – a man who keeps himself in very good shape and spends large amounts of money on his clothes to give a sleek outward appearance – would be portrayed by both the designer suits Jamie would be wearing for the role and his toned physique, which would, of course, be displayed in the nude sex scenes everyone was expecting to see in the film.

The hardest part for Jamie didn't seem to be those scenes where he was nude – instead, the awkward ones were when he was dressed up as the multi millionaire businessman. 'I'm quite awkward in a suit because I don't have an opportunity to wear a suit very often,' he commented, 'and this is a guy who lives in a suit – the best suit. That has to have an effect. But when you end up in a suit for 80 per cent of the filming process, you become pretty comfortable with it.'

In early July, Twitter and *Fifty Shades* fan-websites went into a frenzy once more when it was announced that they would soon get to see a glimpse of Jamie in the movie's first trailer, which would be shown in cinemas from 24 July, and would also debut on the *Today* show on NBC in the US with Jamie and Dakota answering questions about the movie.

On the day the trailer was released, it was soon the most searched for subject on YouTube and Google. Backed by a slowed down, sexed up version of Beyoncé's hit 'Crazy in Love', the trailer showed teasing glimpses of the movie, including

Ana's first look at Christian's infamous red room (where he practises BDSM) and Jamie shirtless in another scene from the film. In an interview with *Today* on NBC in the US, the co-stars talked about the movie.

Dakota Johnson described the sex scenes as 'technical, more choreographed, it's more of a task' than a fun job, but Jamie added that the pair did have chemistry on screen, mainly because they got on well and trusted each other. After all, faking a sex act for the cameras isn't a natural situation, and as Jamie noted, you really have to have faith in the person you're sharing the scene with.

He joked: 'You have these burly men you don't know well three feet from your face – which isn't how I usually have sex!'

E.L. James also commented on the movie, promising that 'the sex is happening [in the film] and I don't think it is particularly watered down!' Clearly enjoying the fact that her two characters had made it to the big screen, she also added that she was really pleased that from early on she had said that she would like two relative unknowns in the roles, and with the casting of Jamie and Dakota, she had got her wish. With the release of *Fifty Shades of Grey*, of course, Dakota and Jamie would be unknown no longer . . .

New Worlds

S hortly after filming finished on *Fifty Shades of Grey*, Jamie had to hop on a plane to Ireland, to begin filming on a second season of *The Fall*. However, he had to stop over in London first to give a series of interviews for a series he had filmed just before the *Fifty Shades* furore had begun – a drama named *New Worlds* that was to be broadcast on UK's Channel 4 in the spring of 2014.

New Worlds was actually the sequel to a drama called *The Devil's Whore* (shown as *The Devil's Mistress* in the USA). Filmed in South Africa – despite being set in England – it was a four-episode drama made by Channel 4 that was first shown in 2008. Set during the 17th century, it followed the adventures of Angelica Fanshawe during the English Civil War. Born in 1623, Angelica becomes a ward of King Charles I and later marries her childhood friend Harry, with the King's permission. However, the couple get caught up in the revolution as Oliver Cromwell takes control of England, and Harry is executed for surrendering their home to the rebels. The series follows Angelica as she is cast out of court and left destitute, and mixes in real-life historical characters, including Puritan Edward Sexby,

Thomas Rainsborough and politician John Lilburne, with the fictional tale.

Written by Peter Flannery, who had penned the acclaimed serial *Our Friends in the North*, the drama featured an impressive cast, including John Simm as Sexby, Dominic West as Oliver Cromwell, Michael Fassbender as Rainsborough, Peter Capaldi as Charles I, and Andrea Riseborough as Angelica. Despite some historians noting that key historical figures and events of the time had been glossed over or omitted entirely, the series won critical acclaim, with the *Guardian* describing it as 'well written and acted', while the *Independent* said it was 'bodice-rippingly melodramatic' (in a good way). The series went on to win Best Drama series at the 35th Broadcasting Press Guild Television and Radio Awards.

It came as no surprise that Channel 4 wanted to follow up *The Devil's Whore* with some sort of sequel. Four years after the episodes were first broadcast, Channel 4 announced that Peter Flannery and Martine Brant were writing a follow-up, entitled *New Worlds*, which would begin filming in July 2013 ready for broadcast in the spring of 2014.

In August 2013, the cast was announced. Eve Best would be taking over from Andrea Riseborough in the role of Angelica Fanshawe since the series was set two decades later, and she would be joined by *Skins* actress Freya Mavor, *Beautiful Creatures* star Alice Englert, *Game Of Thrones* actor Joe Dempsie and Jamie Dornan. '*New Worlds* is a compelling four-part drama capturing the political struggles of the period following the English Civil War, both at home and overseas,' said Channel 4's Head of Drama, Piers Wenger. 'The combination of Peter and Martine's scripts and Charles Martin's direction has attracted a diverse and glittering cast and we're greatly looking forward to seeing their work brought to the screen.'

When asked about the idea for the series, co-writer Martine Brant commented: 'We wanted to tell and celebrate those English men and women who had fought and died for those liberties that we take for granted today. It's [for] those liberties that the rest of the world looks at us with envy.' As director Charles Martin added: 'The Tudors seem to get done to death on television, and we see Victorian England has also been done to death but the Stuarts haven't been covered and yet politically it is the birth of the power of parliament.'

'Popular history has kind of got stuck with this view of the Merry Monarch,' writer Peter Flannery added, about how we view Charles II – and how he wouldn't be seen that way in the new series. 'It was actually a massively turbulent period,' agreed Brant. 'The civil war was particularly ghastly.'

'It's set about 90 years before the American Revolution, and the seeds of dissent and discontent with the English crown were the birth of that,' said Martin.

'We really see how the American dream had been brutalised and sought from the very beginning,' Jamie's co-star Alice Englert added in a behind-the-scenes interview during filming.

The four-part series followed two sets of people in the 1680s as their lives entwine. Firstly, there is a group of settlers in the New World, including young Hope (Englert) and Ned (Joe Dempsie), who live in fear that King Charles II's enforcers in America will uncover Cromwell sympathisers among them, while also facing the threat of Native Americans none too pleased that Charles has given away their land to the unwelcome settlers. Meanwhile, in Oxfordshire in England, Beth, the daughter of *Devil's Whore* Angelica Fanshawe, realises her safe and wealthy life in the countryside is lived alongside people in abject poverty who work as virtual slaves to local landowners and businessmen. And the man who opens her eyes to this other life is outlaw Abe Goffe, the son of one of the men who signed King Charles I's death warrant.

On the set of the series, art director Kevin Woodhouse talked about the look of the world Jamie would be inhabiting in his role as Abe. 'We don't want to be slavish in our accuracy, as essentially we're here to tell a story, and the story comes first.' A model was created of the settlers' village in America before the set itself was built, and the crew researched the costumes, hairstyles and manners of the era

Meanwhile, stunt co-ordinator Gordon Seed was brought in for the fight scenes, which included a raid by Native Americans on the village. Such scenes had their own problems. 'Because the Americans are bare-chested, we can't put squibs on them to shoot blood as there are no costumes to hide them in,' he commented, 'so we're going to shoot paint balls at them!' He went on to explain that for stabbing wounds 'we have tubes in the knives that spurt blood out – during this period there are no fighting styles, just horrible, ugly, gruesome killing.'

David Johnson was in charge of locations, and used Wells Cathedral, street locations in Bristol and Bath, the Elizabethan manor house Chavenage House in the Cotswolds and Chepstow Castle in Monmouthshire, while countryside in Wales doubled for Massachusetts in New England. 'I knew the countryside around the Bristol area quite well,' Jamie remembered, 'but the historical buildings, especially those used for Fanshawe House, were beautiful and that sense of period and atmosphere along with the costume all really help when you are getting into character. We were very lucky to spend the hot summer in those parts of the country and it seemed every day we were in a new stunning spot.'

Part of the appeal of the series for Jamie was that *New Worlds* was being filmed in the UK during the summer of 2013, so he could be near his pregnant wife Amelia, as he told *TV Times* reporter Adrian Lobb.

It was also pretty fun to run around in period costume and to play the role of an outlaw who, in one pivotal scene, attempts to shoot King Charles II himself. (Of course, history tells us Charles died of an illness at the age of 44, so we know Jamie's character Abe doesn't succeed.)

'Annoyingly the failure to kill the king is written in the script, which is a real shame,' Jamie laughed to Lobb. 'The king was well within range and Abe is a good shot. But yes, history is against us. It was an important scene to get right though, and very tricky in this costume. It's not just all the hair extensions, it's the layers. When you're getting your costumes fitted and trying everything on, you're like, "Can I try the hat as well? And that extra tunic?"'

It was clear that Jamie loved the chance to play Abe, despite the restricting costumes, because the character is so passionate about his cause, and everything he does is for a definite reason and belief that he has. As he told the *TV Times*, Abe has made a choice to be an outlaw, and he has decided that if the monarchy is going to be tyrannical, it shouldn't be there.

In another interview, with Serena Davis of the *Telegraph*, he explained more about the role. 'Abe's a character who has sacrificed pretty much everything in his life,' Jamie said, scratching the beard he grew for the role. 'Including a razor!'

'I think he [Abe] is broken,' Jamie told *Interview Magazine* reporter Elvis Mitchell. 'I see broken people as those who have been through hardship – whether it's really ugly hardship like abandonment, abuse, something definitively life altering, like Christian Grey. But there are reasons for these people being the way they are, and that's what drives them.' He went on to tell Mitchell that Abe feels he has suffered injustice due to the fact that his father was one of the men who signed the death warrant for King Charles I, tainting Abe for life. His character does go through changes during the four-part drama, however – to begin with he is a man who talks with his fists. But as time goes on, his character realises that words may be better than actions. In fact, Jamie used some of his friends as inspiration – headstrong pals who, much like Abe, are often aggressive, especially when they are around unfamiliar people.

The role did have its downside, as Abe also has to be a competent horseman. 'I'm actually allergic to horses,' Jamie laughed. 'So I'm quite drugged up on antihistamines when I'm trying to shoot the king. Maybe that's why I miss!'

The horses didn't always behave, either. 'They're a little cautious about letting actors near horses too much,' he told *What's on TV* magazine. 'Anything widely shot was done with a stunt double. One time, when the horse wasn't behaving for a close up, I ended up on the stuntman's shoulders. The poor guy's got reins on and everything, and I had to sort of wriggle about. I don't know who it was worse for!'

Talking to Channel 4 while filming, Jamie went into more detail about his character. 'Abe is a young, idealistic renegade who is very determined in his fight to make England a true republic and end the tyrannical rule of the Stuarts' throne,' he explained. 'It is a similar fight to that taken up by his father William Goffe who was a real historical figure [while Abe is fictional] and one whom Abe idolises. He is trying to uphold the mantle of his father's campaign and muster up support among others. He is headstrong, too much so at times, and is often quick to use his fists but he learns during the course of the drama that there are better paths of action.'

All this sounds very political, but Jamie added that he thought the action was still relatable to today's audiences. 'I think the themes of *New Worlds* are all ones that young people watching the drama can relate to. Young people still feel enraged about the same injustices, although I like to think in England people now are treated with greater decency and things aren't as brutal and bloody as they were at that time.'

He told reporter Vicki Power that the show wasn't 'medieval porn' like some historical dramas such as *The Tudors*, but that the period the series was set in was far more brutal than he had been aware of. 'Four hundred years [ago] doesn't seem that long to me, yet it's so barbaric – the deaths, the way people treated each other and the way the country was run was quite disturbing.'

Writer Peter Flannery was pleased with Jamie's casting as the fictional son of William Goffe. 'He has enough anger, enough fire in him generally for the part,' Flannery commented, 'and he also has great commitment.'

One of the writers, Martine Brant, suggested that the cast read the book *Cavalier: A Tale of Chivalry, Passion and Great Houses* by historian and TV presenter Lucy Worsley, as research for their roles. 'Freya [Jamie's co-star] and I both read it. It became a joke competition between Freya and I to finish it. My copy was more subtly on my iPad but Freya constantly lugged her copy around everywhere as I teased and tested her knowledge!' Jamie laughed. Much of what he read was new to him, as the English Civil War hadn't featured much in history lessons at his school in Belfast, and it cames as a surprise to learn what a barbaric and bloody time in history it was.

While the role was just as bloody as playing a serial killer in *The Fall* – in the second episode of *New Worlds*, Abe is shot and has a rather nasty bullet wound that has to (gulp) be sealed with a red-hot poker – it was something of a departure for Jamie to be playing a romantic lead.

'Although Beth [Abe's love interest] was born into a family embroiled in the turmoil of the Civil War . . . she has been protected by her mother Angelica, and Abe initially finds her naivety frustrating. Abe resents that she has grown up in such a protected, safe way in this commonwealth environment created by her mother, when he has chosen to face the much tougher realities around them,' Jamie explained. 'He doesn't understand how she can't see her life is an illusion. They are classic star-crossed lovers to start with but ultimately they can't help themselves. As we all know, love is a very powerful thing!'

He paused. 'I have to say it was nice to play a romantic hero, especially after *The Fall* where I had to apologise to pretty much every actress after each shot was filmed!'

However, both he and co-star Joe Dempsie, whose own character had a romance on screen with Alice Englert, were slightly nervous about filming love scenes. 'Joe and I watched all the *Sex and the City* box sets,' he joked, 'twice! That helped!'

Jamie's co-star Freya Mavor talked about working with him as her romantic lead. 'One of Jamie's brilliant traits is that he doesn't take himself too seriously. He takes the job seriously but he made being on set so much fun and between heart-breaking scenes we could goof around which was really easy,' she smiled. 'We became great friends, which I think really helped us play Beth and Abe, who are not only in love but also see each other as comrades and support each other. And he is gorgeous which helps as well!'

There was clearly camaraderie on set between the four leading actors, Jamie, Freya, Alice Englert and Joe Dempsie, and when they were reunited for a photo shoot with *Glamour* magazine to promote the series, they all laughed and joked, especially when asked to describe their fellow actors in just three words.

'Wise, uncle, friend' was how Alice described Joe, while Alice was called 'kooky, funky, aunt' by Freya. Jamie got to choose his words for Freya – 'Scottish, kind and irritating' while Joe ended by using three words to describe Jamie that caused the other cast members to crack up laughing: 'Ow my shoulder!'

Joe's comment referred to Jamie's shoulder injury that he had had two surgeries on since 2013. 'I've got a dodgy shoulder,' he told *TV Choice* magazine when they asked about it. 'I've had two surgeries since *The Fall* finished, so luckily there isn't too much physical fighting [in *New Worlds*]. I was skiing a few years back and I did something stupid. In *The Fall* they hid it well and we shot around it but I couldn't lift my left arm up above a certain point and I was on a lot of painkillers.

When we finished and I realised how bloody sore it was, I decided to get it fixed, so I've had two surgeries since and it's still not quite right!'

While having fun with Jamie it was clear that his co-stars weren't put off by his new celebrity status as the man who would be Christian Grey, and in an interview with the *Daily Express* in March 2014 to promote *New Worlds* being shown on TV, it was clear Jamie was yet to be affected by his new-found fame.

'Nothing's changed. I don't get recognised much, except once when somebody shouted "There's that serial killer!" at me, which provoked an interesting reaction as people began to panic,' he said, having been recognised not for Christian, but for his role in *The Fall*. '*The Fall* has changed the landscape of my professional career slightly,' he added, 'but I know so many actors who don't work and a few who work a lot. I'm just happy to do good work.'

As *New Worlds* aired on Channel 4 in the UK and around the world, it seemed that more work was coming in thick and fast, including a return to Paul Spector and the lead role in a romantic Belgian drama . . .

The Future

While fans eagerly counted down the days, weeks and months until *Fifty Shades of Grey* would be released on Valentine's weekend 2015, new dad Jamie was kept busy, not only with a new film and TV series to work on, but also because spring traditionally means awards season – the time of year when Oscars, BAFTAs and other acting accolades are handed out.

Awards are handed out for the previous year's work, so during the 2014 season, it was TV series from 2013 that were nominated – and this included Jamie Dornan and Gillian Anderson's acclaimed thriller, *The Fall*. They – and the producers and directors of the series – faced some serious competition, as 2013 had been a superb year for TV drama, especially in the UK. Two of the most watched and praised dramas that *The Fall* would be competing against were also gritty British dramas – *Southcliffe* and *Broadchurch*.

Southcliffe told the story of the effect of a series of shootings in a small English town by local man Stephen Morton, as played by Sean Harris, and the impact they have on the community. Harris was praised for his performance as the killer, whom we follow before and after the tragedy. The cast also included Rory Kinnear as a journalist covering the story, and Jamie's *New Worlds* co-star Joe Dempsie as a young soldier who beats up Morton, triggering his shooting spree.

Meanwhile, *Broadchurch* – like *The Fall* – had become one of the most talked about series of 2013. A crime drama set on the Dorset coast, it followed detectives Alec Hardy (David Tennant) and Ellie Miller (Olivia Colman) as they investigated the death of an 11-year-old boy.

It was in March 2014 that the first awards of the UK TV season took place – the Broadcasting Press Guild Awards. Voted for by a collection of journalists who specialise in writing and broadcasting about television and the media, the 2014 nominations included *The Fall* for Best Drama Series, competing against *Broadchurch* and the Jane Campion drama *Top of the Lake*, while Gillian Anderson was nominated for her role in *The Fall* as Best Actress, alongside Olivia Colman for *Broadchurch*, Elisabeth Moss for *Top of the Lake* and Maxine Peake for *The Village*. *The Fall* was also nominated for Best Writer (Allan Cubitt) again up against the writers of *Broadchurch* and *Top of the Lake*, while Jamie was nominated for the Breakthrough Award, alongside actress Sharon Rooney for the comedy *My Mad Fat Diary* and BT Sport for their TV channel launch.

Unfortunately, *Broadchurch* won Best Drama Series, and also beat out *The Fall* in the Best Writer and Best Actress categories. But the winner of the Breakthrough Award was Jamie Dornan for *The Fall*. Unable to attend the ceremony in person, he accepted his prize by video, dressed in a tan jacket and sporting a beard that looked slightly familiar, as he went on to explain.

'Thank you to the Broadcasting Press Guild for this award – it means a lot,' he said to the camera. 'Professionally speaking, *The Fall* was the best thing that ever happened to me, so the fact that so many of you guys felt the same and responded so well to it, as I had so much fun making it, so that's very pleasing. I usually don't need much of an excuse to have a drink in the afternoon, so I would have loved to have been with you there today but unfortunately we're filming the second series of *The Fall* over in Belfast so that's the reason I can't be there but I am really touched by this and I thank you very much.'

Yes, Jamie was back in Belfast filming a second series of *The Fall*. There had been speculation that a second season was on the cards as soon as the TV ratings for the first season were in – as BBC2's highest-rated drama in eight years it was almost a forgone conclusion that a follow-up should be made, especially as the first series had ended on something of a cliffhanger, with detective Stella Gibson still on the trail of murderer Paul Spector.

In October 2013, the UK's TV Wise website reported that a second season of *The Fall* would be made in 2014, this time with writer Allan Cubitt behind the camera as first-season director Jakob Verbruggen would not be returning. Jamie and Gillian definitely would be, however, and they would be joined by Archie Panjabi, Gerard McCarthy and Emmet J. Scanlan. It was then announced in spring 2014, just before *The Fall 2* started filming, that the cast would be joined by *Merlin* star Colin Morgan, who would be playing DS Tom Anderson, one of the officers involved in the search for serial killer Spector.

'I'm delighted to be joining the cast of *The Fall* for what is going to be an exciting and gripping second series,' Morgan commented. 'Allan Cubitt has written exceptional material and I feel very privileged to be working with him and the very talented cast.'

The second series would pick up from where the first season ended, with Stella Gibson forced to take greater risks in pursuit of Spector when he trespasses into her private world, delighting in taunting and provoking her. Her only hope is discovering some clues in Spector's past that may help the investigation.

'I'm over the moon to be back in production with this team again and to step into the shoes of the elusive Stella for what promises to be an even darker second season,' Gillian Anderson said from the set, while Jamie added, 'I'm delighted to be back in production for the second series of *The Fall*. Allan Cubitt has outdone himself, and the scripts are stunning.'

Ben Stephenson, the BBC Controller of Drama Commissioning, also commented on the news there would be a second series. '*The Fall* has proved both a critical and ratings hit for BBC Two and another reminder of the resurgence of drama on the channel. With more of Allan Cubitt's intricate and thrilling plot revelations yet to unfold through the captivating performances of Gillian and Jamie, a second series is a must. Obviously we can't give too much away . . . but what we can say is it will be as surprising and intense as the first.'

In an interview with *TV Times* magazine in March 2014, Jamie suggested that the new series may actually be filmed in a new location rather than the Belfast of the first series. 'After his killing spree in Northern Ireland, Paul Spector is coming to get *you*, Scotland,' he teased, building on the fact that his character was last seen heading in that direction at the end of the first season. Certainly, Jamie couldn't wait to see how the story progressed, adding, 'It's lovely to know you're going on to something that was received well, and a character you love playing.'

Gillian Anderson was full of praise for Jamie's return, scotching any rumours that he wouldn't be back due to his role in *Fifty Shades of Grey*. 'Jamie is just the sweetest, nicest guy you could ever meet,' she told the *Belfast Telegraph*, 'and no, he hasn't changed at all. Of course he will be back! You know, if he says he is leaving us, I'll give him a good slap and change his mind!'

Bronagh Waugh, who plays Paul Spector's wife in both series of *The Fall*, confirmed that Jamie's big upcoming part hadn't changed him between the filming of the first and second series. 'He's just Jamie. When you're an actor and you work on the set all the time, it's just a work thing,' she told *IN!* magazine about the *Fifty Shades* sex symbol she has had to share love scenes with. 'Our intimate scenes are the least intimate moments ever. For a start, there are 40 people in the room. I remember we did this one scene in the bath and the water had to be still, no bubbles. I got in and lay down and I see Jamie's shoulders going like this [she shakes], and I look down and there's my modesty cover floating down the bath! So when things like that happen, it's the most unromantic, un-sexy thing ever.'

Fans would have to wait until the autumn of 2014 for the second series to appear on British TV, while the cast filmed in Belfast during May and June to get the series ready. Stephen Wright of BBC Northern Ireland said: 'It is fantastic to have production on series two of *The Fall* up and running in

Belfast. We were delighted with the response to series one and can't wait to unleash Allan Cubitt's superb new scripts on the audience.'

Co-star Gerard McCarthy was cornered on the red carpet of the Raindance Film Festival in London for more information and he revealed what little he could about the new series. 'It's actually more intense than the first season which is a bit of a claim. It's more of the same, but even *more* of the same! The scripts were incredible and we have Allan Cubitt, who wrote it and is also directing this season, so it's a real journey into his sick twisted mind!'

McCarthy was asked what Jamie was like now that he had many female fans due to his casting in *Fifty Shades*. 'It's interesting, because there aren't many people on this show that work with Jimmy apart from the girl who plays his wife, but he's an absolute gent and a joy to work with and he's just a really, really lovely guy, and I think the entire cast of *The Fall* were just delighted for him that his career just took a massive, massive leap forward this year – it was brilliant. He can't say anything about the film but we will all be there en masse when it comes out and we'll mock and tease him after we've seen the film!'

Jamie himself was interviewed on the set of *The Fall 2* by BBC Newsline Northern Ireland and chatted about returning to play Paul Spector. 'It's not a breeze to play him, but I relish it and I love it and I've said this in the past – I approach Spector as two different characters, because I think that makes the most sense and it makes it easiest for me to relate to what I was doing in either killing mode or family mode – both equally difficult to play.'

He also chatted about returning to his hometown to work and how lovely it was to be back in Belfast, especially as he could now enjoy, as an adult, the city in which he went to school.

Jamie was asked in *Interview Magazine* if he could reveal anything that would be happening in the follow-up season of *The Fall* and he hinted that viewers would perhaps learn why Spector is the way he is, maybe by some revelation about his past. Certainly, the role of Spector would be developed further than was possible in the first season.

'It's been over two years – I haven't stayed in his mind for the entire two years, don't worry – but when I'm in it, I do feel very comfortable in his skin, and that can only lead to rare things happening. We're going to see more of Spector, but in a slightly different light. I can't say too much more than that!'

Jamie also talked about watching the first season before he began work on the second, even though he didn't enjoy watching himself. As one of the stars, it was awkward for him to watch his scenes, but he admitted he would have loved the show as a thriller if he hadn't been in it, as the story is so good, and the other performances – especially his co-star Gillian Anderson's – were so gripping as well.

Jamie may have felt discomfort watching himself but his role as Paul Spector had clearly appealed to viewers and critics alike, as was evidenced with the announcement of more awards nominations in April 2014. On 5 April, the Irish Film and Television Academy held their 11th annual awards in Dublin, following the announcement of the award nominations in February. *The Fall* was nominated for Best Drama – competing against fantasy adventure *Game of Thrones*, Irish crime drama *Love/Hate* and the Gabriel Byrne-starring *Quirke*, while Jamie was nominated for his lead role, competing with Byrne, Chris O'Dowd for *Moone Boy* and Tom Vaughan Lawlor for *Love/Hate*. *The Fall* was also nominated in the Director of Photography, Make-Up & Hair, Original Score and Production Design categories.

Jamie attended the awards at the DoubleTree Hilton in Dublin along with well-known names such as Michael Fassbender, Colin Farrell, Steve Coogan, director Neil Jordan and Jeremy Irons. He watched *The Fall* win Best Drama and Original Score, and then Jamie, looking dashing in a dinner suit and black bow tie, heard actress Fionnula Flanagan read out the winner of the Best Actor award – and it was him.

'Thank you to everyone who worked on *The Fall*, it's the best professional thing that's ever happened to me,' he said, echoing his acceptance speech for the Broadcasting Press Guild awards. 'Thank you to Allan Cubitt for creating it, for taking a massive punt on putting me in the driving seat. He took a lot of risks and had to convince a lot of people, and I'm very grateful for that.'

Jamie's night wasn't over, however. Jeremy Irons later announced the prize for Rising Star, and it was Jamie's turn once again to leave his table and accept the award to many cheers. 'Thank you very much, there are some massively important people I forgot to thank before! I want to thank my beautiful family for being really beautiful, my wife who is the best thing that ever happened to me. I want to thank our baby who is four months old and asleep upstairs, and I want to thank everyone who I didn't thank the first time from *The Fall*. I want to thank everyone who's ever met me and been nice to me, I guess, thanks a million!'

He was obviously thrilled but also a little overawed by the experience, and just a few weeks later on 18 May it was time for him to walk the red carpet again, this time for the prestigious BAFTA Television Awards in London. The nominees had been announced on 7 April, with Jamie nominated in the Leading Actor category alongside Sean Harris from *Southcliffe*, Luke Newberry from the supernatural drama *In the Flesh* and Dominic West for *Burton and Taylor* in which he had played the legendary actor Richard Burton. *The Fall* was also nominated for Best Mini Series (alongside *Southcliffe*, *In the Flesh* and *The Great Train Robbery*). Alas, on this occasion, neither Jamie nor the series won (Sean Harris and *In the Flesh* took home the awards), but he clearly had a great time on the red carpet chatting to fans, with his wife Amelia Warner, in a pretty cream lace trapeze dress, happy at his side.

'It's your first BAFTA nomination,' interviewer Jenni Falconer asked him outside the event. 'First and last, probably,' Jamie humbly joked. 'You can't really prepare for something like this, you sort of go along with the madness and try and enjoy yourself,' he added, looking at the throngs of people taking his photograph. 'This could only happen to me once so it is fun to be involved in it.'

She also asked him whether he thought his success in *The Fall* was affecting his career more than his upcoming role in *Fifty Shades of Grey*. 'I have no idea yet, until *Fifty* comes out, it's hard to know how that's going to have an effect on me. *The Fall* changed everything in that I'd never done a job for the BBC before, never mind the lead in something as well put together as this . . .'

It did seem that Jamie's whole professional life was on hold until the release of *Fifty Shades of Grey* in 2015, since it was the role everyone wanted to talk about, especially when Jamie and Dakota Johnson were seen flying back to Vancouver in October 2014 to reshoot some scenes for the film. Rumour had it that the reshoots were to add a bit more sizzle to the movie to match its sexy source material, but since cast and crew weren't allowed to talk about *Fifty Shades*, it was just speculation. With the second season of *The Fall* debuting on British TV just a few weeks later, journalists interviewing Jamie for the series were given strict instructions not to ask him about his highly anticipated movie role.

He was happy to talk about *The Fall*'s second series, of course, and thrilled that it was one of the most talked about returning shows on TV. 'Quite far in advance I got a very detailed, 80 page breakdown of what would happen in each episode and I was shaking,' he told the BBC. In an interview with the *Daily Telegraph* as the series aired, Jamie noted there was one difference he experienced in returning to the role of serial killer Paul Spector – during the first series, Jamie was playing a man who was a father, but by the time filming started on the second season, he was a father himself. 'At the time [of the first series] I couldn't relate to being a father, but I can now,' he said. 'It humanises him for me . . . if you only ever saw him inside the sickness of his mind, the audience would never be on his side, and I think that is the most chilling aspect of it.' Jamie even hinted that season two may not spell the end for his character, teasing *TV Times* magazine by saying: 'I'm loyal, and if they want to keep writing Spector, I'm in. That is, if Spector is still around . . .'

Frenzy about *The Fall 2* reached fever pitch in the first week of November 2014, with Jamie voted Vertu Breakthrough Artist by GQ magazine, one of the few titles that got him to reveal something – anything – about his role in *Fifty Shades of Grey*. 'In some ways, it'll break a few boundaries,' he revealed. 'But at the same time, they want to put bums on seats. They can't alienate an audience – it has to be watchable, it can't be hardcore!' Even Gillian Anderson, being interviewed by *Red* magazine for *The Fall*, was asked about her sexy co-star's very famous upcoming role. 'On the first series, people were like, "Who is this guy? Is he an ex-model or something?" Now people don't ever want to talk to me about *The X-Files*. They only want to ask about Jamie Dornan!' Indeed, Charlotte Sinclair, in her interview with Jamie for *Vogue*'s November 2014 issue, noted that all her friends wanted to come along to the interview with her, as well as half of the *Vogue* staff. 'It's actually too insane,' he told her about his new found fame thanks to *Fifty Shades*. 'They're very loved books, but they are just books, and we're just trying to make a film.'

Chatting to Nigel Farndale of the *Observer* (once again to promote *The Fall* but with the conversation turning to THAT movie), Jamie admitted that while E.L. James' books are loved, neither he nor wife Amelia had actually read them. He added, however, that while he didn't read the books, for research he went to a BDSM dungeon in Vancouver and watched 'a perfectly sweet and normal woman' being spanked.

Speaking for Jamie's many fans perhaps, Farndale also asked just how much audiences could expect to see of Jamie in the movie – 'there were contracts in place that said that viewers wouldn't be seeing my, um, todger . . .' – with him noting that he's glad that's in place, because he is worried enough about the ribbing all his old friends are going to give him when they see the film anyway.

As fans settled down to watch *The Fall 2* – while counting the three months to go before the release of *Fifty Shades* – Jamie had another movie on the horizon that would show there was more to him than a sex symbol or even a serial killer: he could also be a romantic lead, thanks to the Belgian drama *Flying Home*.

Written and directed by Belgian director Dominique Deruddere, *Flying Home* is a Belgian and English language drama co-starring British actor Anthony Head and Charlotte De Bruyne. Filmed in September 2012 and released in Belgium in April 2014 (with other international releases planned for the future), it's the story of an American corporate raider, Colin (played by Jamie), who is trying to impress a potential client, a wealthy Arab sheikh who is a passionate pigeon fancier. He has been trying to buy a champion pigeon from Flanders, but the owner Jos Pauwels refuses to sell. To gain the sheikh's business, Colin proposes that if he can convince the Flemish owner to sell the bird, the sheikh must sign with his company. Of course, when Colin arrives in Flanders, pretending to be a teacher looking for the grave of a relative who died in the First World War, he falls for Pauwels' granddaughter Isabelle (De Bruyne), complicating his trip.

'The story of *Flying Home* is based around my character, called Colin Montgomery, and he works for a powerful financing group in New York and he's trying to get the investment of a sheikh over in Dubai, and the sheikh will only invest in his company if he can get hold of this pigeon!' Jamie explained from the set. 'My character takes it upon himself to get over to Belgium and get that pigeon no matter what it takes. Along the way he becomes taken with Belgium and the people in it, so he is torn between what is right and what is wrong.

'Pigeon fancying is something I knew absolutely nothing about, but it's quite an interesting world. There's a lot of money to be made from it which is something I wasn't aware of,' he continued. 'The only person I ever knew who did it was Mike Tyson, the former world heavyweight champion of the world. He is into pigeon fancying in a big way, so I guess if someone as high profile as that who is as aggressive as that is into something as obscure as pigeon fancying it must be worth something.'

It was very different from any other movie Jamie had worked on, as many of the cast and crew were Flemish. This made for a relaxed working atmosphere, with people chattering in different languages, including French, Flemish and English and, best of all, the promise of a beer at the end of each working day!

Director Dominique Deruddere talked about the casting of Jamie, before he was a well-known name. Dominique had received a lot of résumés and tapes from the British casting agent on the movie, Kate Dowd, featuring young actors who all fit the profile of 'handsome and successful'. 'No one appeared to have that second layer which is so necessary for the main character. Jamie has more than his pretty boy look at first revealed. I was immediately interested, and when I saw a scene from *The Fall* that was sent to me, I made the decision. Jamie has managed to convey the increasing doubt and struggle of the main character with a lot of nuance and talent.'

He then added: 'He's an actor of whom we – because of *Fifty*

Shades of Grey – will hear a lot of in the future around the world, and I am delighted that two Belgian directors, Jakob Verbruggen [of the first series of *The Fall*] and myself might have been at the cradle of a great career.'

Deruddere had uttered what many of Jamie's former co-stars and directors had been thinking – that they had crossed paths with someone who would soon become one of the most sought after actors in the world.

With his wife Amelia and daughter (whose privacy he protects so fiercely he has refused even to reveal her name) by his side, and the role of a lifetime in his hands at the age of just 32, it seems that the young Irish boy from Holywood had captured Hollywood's heart. But instead of planning his next blockbuster role, Jamie had more important things on his mind for the future.

'Right now I don't need to work if there's nothing I want to do,' he told the *Guardian* in the spring of 2014. 'I've done three jobs back to back. Let's see how they are received. If there's nothing I want to do, I'll just play golf and change nappies.'

He wasn't joking about the golf, either. At the start of October 2014, Jamie competed in the Alfred Dunhill Links Championship in Scotland with golfer Danny Willett; they played against golfers Rory McIlroy and Colin Montgomerie, celebrities including singer Huey Lewis, sportsmen Steve Redgrave and Tim Henman, and actors Damien Lewis, Hugh Grant and Bill Murray.

'This week is a bit of a rest,' Jamie told website *Daily Record* from the golf course. 'It's been good fun with Bill Murray. He's a legend with a great swing and he can't stay serious for too long and he was great company. It was jokes all round until I was hitting it so badly I couldn't really stand for jokes anymore!'

A quiet life of golf and family didn't last long however. By the end of 2014, Jamie – who had been working non-stop for over a year – signed on to not one, but two new movies. He had already filmed a comedy drama originally called *Chef* (its name was soon dropped, due to the Jon Favreau film of the same name) during the summer of 2014, in between *Fifty Shades* and *The Fall*. Starring Bradley Cooper as a chef returning to London to win a coveted Michelin star, the film had Jamie joining a cast that also included Emma Thompson, Sienna Miller, Uma Thurman and Matthew Rhys.

It was then announced that he would play the lead role in *The Siege of Jadotville*, due to film in the summer of 2015 – a military drama centering around the true story of the siege of 150 Irish UN troops, led by Commandant Pat Quinlan, in the Congo in 1961.

Jamie would star as the commandant whose men held out against three thousand local troops. 'I can't wait to get stuck into *Jadotville*,' Jamie said of the film, which would shoot in Ireland and South Africa. 'It's an unbelievable story and Commandant Pat Quinlan is going to be a treat of a character to tackle.'

He also signed up for the movie *The Ninth Life of Louis Drax*, based on the novel by Liz Jensen. Originally set to be made into a movie by director Anthony Minghella shortly before his sudden death in 2008, the 2004 suspense novel tells the story of nine-year-old Louis, a bright, precocious, accident-prone problem child who falls off a cliff into a ravine and is left in a deep coma. While his father vanishes and his mother is paralysed with shock, it is left to a doctor, Pascal Dannachet, to try to coax Louis back to consciousness. However, instead the doctor is drawn into a mystery that tests the boundaries of fantasy and reality.

Jamie was cast in the lead role – now renamed Dr Allan Pascal – while Max Minghella (son of Anthony) wrote the script and Alexandre Aja (best known for the horror *Mirrors*, with Kiefer Sutherland, and *Horns* with Daniel Radcliffe) signed on to direct. In a statement announcing the movie, Max Minghella said: 'Tim [Bricknell, one of the producers of the film] and I are thrilled this deeply personal project is being brought to fruition with passion and integrity.'

As the most eagerly awaited film of his career loomed on the horizon, 2015 was shaping up nicely for Jamie Dornan. Happily married and the father of a one-year-old daughter, Hollywood's hottest new movie star could look forward to exciting new projects as well as two possible sequels to *Fifty Shades of Grey*. Or maybe not? 'I'm not getting naked,' he told *Vogue* in November 2014. 'I'm sick of it. Sick of it.' Millions of fans, though, would surely disagree . . .

Timeline

1 May 1982

James Dornan is born in Belfast to mother Lorna and father James. He is their third child, following two daughters.

4 June 1982

Amelia Warner is born in Liverpool to actress Annette Ekblom and actor Alun Lewis.

1996

Jamie writes to his great-aunt, actress Greer Garson, but discovers she died on April 6.

1998

Jamie's mother, Lorna, dies of pancreatic cancer.

Jamie and school friend David Alexander form the band Sons of Jim (so named because both their fathers' names are Jim). The pair write and perform folk songs in their spare time.

1999

Four of Jamie's friends are killed in a car crash near County Down.

July 2001

Amelia Warner 'marries' actor Colin Farrell in Tahiti but the marriage isn't legally recognised. The pair split four months later in November 2001.

2002

Channel 4 launch a TV talent show for models called *Model Behaviour* in 2001. Jamie is posted by a Belfast modelling agency and asked to try out for the second series of the show. He doesn't make the final cut, but is offered modelling work with renowned photographer Bruce Weber.

Jamie's dad marries Samina, his second wife.

August 2003

Jamie is hired to shoot a modelling campaign for the jewellers Asprey. The shoot is in New York and it is there that he meets actress Keira Knightley and they begin dating.

2004

Jamie is named the new face – and body – of Calvin Klein.

Jamie and Keira are photographed together at the launch of Asprey's flagship store in New York.

2005

Jamie's photo campaigns include shoots for Armani Exchange and *GQ* magazine and he becomes the face of Dior Homme's winter campaign.

Summer 2005

Jamie and Keira announce that they have split up. 'Keira and

Jamie have decided to call a halt to their relationship in its current phase, but they remain completely committed to each other as friends and will continue to see each other in this capacity.'

It is announced that Sofia Coppola will be making a movie in France about the life of Marie Antoinette.

September 2005

Jamie and David release songs on their label Doorstep Records including a Sons of Jim EP featuring the song 'Fairytale'.

7 October 2005

Sons of Jim perform on *The Kelly Show* in Belfast, presented by TV chat show host Gerry Kelly. The boys perform the folk ballad 'Fairytale'.

November 2005

While rehearsing with bandmate David Alexander, Jamie is called and told there may be a part for him in the movie *Marie Antoinette*. He travels to Paris to audition and is offered the role of Axel Von Fersen, lover of Marie, the next day.

2006

Photo shoots in 2006 include Gap, H&M, Dior Homme and the Calvin Klein campaign featuring a topless Kate Moss.

May 2006

Sons of Jim perform at Islington Academy in London and also at the opening of the Vans store in Carnaby Street.

Marie Antoinette premieres at the Cannes Film Festival to mixed reviews.

October 2006
Jamie travels to New York for the New York Film Festival, where *Marie Antoinette* is well received.

November 2006
Jamie is interviewed by Guy Trebay for the *New York Times*. The interview is entitled 'The Golden Torso', and Jim Moore also calls Jamie the male Kate Moss.

September 2007
Jamie films his first lead role, as soldier Ed in the Hammer horror *Beyond the Rave*. The shoot takes place in Buckinghamshire and Plumstead, East London.

Spring 2008
Jamie films the small-scale drama *Shadows in the Sun* with renowned actress Jean Simmons.

April 2008
Beyond the Rave premieres on MySpace.

Late 2008
Sons of Jim split up.

2009
Jamie shoots the Calvin Klein underwear campaign in Palm Springs that also features actress Eva Mendes. His shoots

this year also include campaigns for Armani Jeans and Aquascutum.

Shadows in the Sun wins two awards at the 2009 WorldFest Houston for Best Screenplay and the Special Jury Award for Best Film.

Summer 2009

Calvin Klein launches the '9 Countries, 9 Men, 1 Winner' competition to find a new male model and Jamie is one of the judges, along with Klein and Select Model Management, who choose Englishman Laurence Cope.

August 2009

A TV producer by the name of Erika Mitchell begins writing fan fiction based on the *Twilight* novels. These evolve into a story named *Master of the Universe*.

Late 2010

The producers of *Once Upon a Time*, a new fantasy TV series, begin casting for the lead roles.

January 2011

Erika Mitchell signs a print-on-demand and e-book contract with The Writer's Coffee Shop. Her first novel, *Fifty Shades of Grey*, based on her fan fiction *Master of the Universe*, is published. The sequel, *Fifty Shades Darker*, follows in September 2011.

Summer 2011

Jamie wins the roles of the sheriff and the Huntsman in the

TV series *Once Upon a Time* and begins filming in Vancouver. The episode that features his character throughout is 'The Heart is a Lonely Hunter' and it is broadcast in the US in December 2011.

Late 2011
Jamie Dornan begins dating singer/actress Amelia Warner.

February 2012
BBC Drama announce a new TV thriller is to be made called *The Fall*. Gillian Anderson is confirmed as the lead actress.

March 2012
Erika Mitchell – now known by her pen name E.L. James – signs a deal for her *Fifty Shades* books to be published worldwide by Vintage Books. Deadline.com reports that ten movie studio chiefs are rumoured to be battling it out for the film rights to the books.

26 March 2012
Jamie is confirmed as the lead male actor in *The Fall*. He is cast as Paul Spector, 'a serial killer who is terrorising the city of Belfast.'

June 2012
Filming finishes on the first season of *The Fall*.

Summer 2012
Fifty Shades of Grey becomes a publishing phenomenon.

September 2012

He films the Belgian movie *Flying Home* in Belgium, but it is not released until 2014.

October 2012

Kelly Marcel is announced as the screenwriter for the *Fifty Shades of Grey* movie adaptation.

Late 2012

Jamie films a return for Sheriff Graham in the season two episode of *Once Upon a Time*, called 'Welcome To Storybrooke'. The episode is broadcast in the US in the spring of 2013.

26 April 2013

It is announced that Jamie and Amelia are married, following a quiet family ceremony in Somerset.

13 May 2013

The first episode of *The Fall* is broadcast in the UK. A total of 3.5 million viewers tune into BBC2, making the series the highest-rated drama launch on the channel for almost eight years.

19 June 2013

E.L. James announced via Twitter that a director had been hired for *Fifty Shades of Grey*: 'I'm delighted & thrilled to let you guys know that Sam Taylor-Johnson has agreed to direct the film of *Fifty Shades of Grey*.'

24 June 2013

Jamie and Amelia confirm that they are expecting a baby. 'Jim [Jamie's dad] and I are delighted that our third grandchild is on the way,' said Samina Dornan [Jamie's stepmother] to *Sunday Life* in Northern Ireland. 'The early wellbeing scanning was a beautiful and emotional experience for all present.' The scan took place at the 3fivetwo Healthcare clinic in Lisburn Road in Belfast and was performed by Samina.

July 2013

Jamie begins filming the historical TV series *New Worlds* for Channel 4. The four-part series is set during the 1680s on both sides of the Atlantic and co-stars Alice Englert and Joe Dempsie. The series is filmed in Bristol, Bath, Wells and the Cotswolds during the summer of 2013.

2 September 2013

E.L. James announced via Twitter the two leads for the *Fifty Shades of Grey* movie. 'I am delighted to let you know that the lovely Dakota Johnson has agreed to be our Anastasia in the film adaptation of *Fifty Shades of Grey*,' she tweeted, and then a few minutes later she sent another tweet. 'The gorgeous and talented Charlie Hunnam will be Christian Grey in the film adaptation of *Fifty Shades of Grey*.'

October 2013

It is announced that there will be a second series of *The Fall*, starring Jamie and Gillian Anderson, to be filmed in the spring of 2014 for an autumn 2014 broadcast.

12 October 2013

It is announced that Charlie Hunnam will no longer be in the *Fifty Shades of Grey* movie. 'The filmmakers of *Fifty Shades of Grey* and Charlie Hunnam have agreed to find another male lead given Hunnam's immersive TV schedule [on *Sons of Anarchy*] which is not allowing him time to adequately prepare for the role of Christian Grey.'

23 October 2013

Jamie Dornan is hired for the role of Christian Grey, after being phoned at 1.30 a.m. in the UK to be offered the role. 'I was sort of pretending I wasn't waiting, but the phone was in my hand, halfway to my ear.'

A casting call for extras is posted, looking for actors to work in Los Angeles and Vancouver on 'The Adventures of Max and Banks', the working title of *Fifty Shades*.

November 2013

Amelia gives birth a baby girl at a hospital in Vancouver. Jamie and Amelia do not release the baby's name or birth date to the press, and news of the birth is not revealed until 16 December.

1 December 2013

Filming begins in Vancouver on *Fifty Shades of Grey*.

21 February 2014

Principal photography finishes on *Fifty Shades of Grey*. E.L. James tweeted 'And that's a wrap . . .' to confirm that filming had ended.

22 February 2014

Jamie is seen leaving Vancouver on a flight bound for London.

March 2014

A list written by Lindsay Lohan is leaked to the press. It names all the celebrities she claims to have slept with, including Jamie and other actors such as Colin Farrell, Orlando Bloom and James Franco.

Jamie begins filming series two of *The Fall* in Belfast.

Jamie wins the Broadcasting Press Guild award for his Breakthrough performance in *The Fall*. He accepts his award by video from the set of *The Fall*.

A teaser trailer for *Fifty Shades of Grey* is shown to the film industry at CinemaCon.

5 April 2014

Jamie attends the Irish Film and Television Academy Awards in Dublin and wins the Best Actor and Rising Star awards during the evening.

6 April 2014

New Worlds is broadcast on Channel 4 in the UK.

18 May 2014

Jamie and Amelia make their first red carpet appearance since the birth of their daughter, at the BAFTA Television Awards in London. Jamie is nominated for Best Actor for *The Fall* but loses out to *Southcliffe* actor Sean Harris.

18 June 2014

The first photo from the set of *Fifty Shades of Grey* is released to the public and features Jamie, as Christian, sat behind the wheel of an Audi R8.

21 July 2014

It is announced that Jamie's next movie will be in a movie tentatively titled *Adam Jones*. Bradley Cooper will star as a chef who returns to London to win a third Michelin star, and Jamie is confirmed as one of his co-stars along with Emma Thompson, Sienna Miller and Lily James. The movie, originally titled *Chef*, is directed by *ER*'s John Wells.

24 July 2014

The *Fifty Shades of Grey* movie trailer is first shown in cinemas worldwide. Fans get a look at Ana and Christian, as played by Dakota Johnson and Jamie Dornan, and see scenes of the movie backed by a special version of 'Crazy in Love' by Beyoncé, recorded for the movie.

Autumn 2014

Series two of *The Fall* is broadcast on TV.

13 February 2015

Fifty Shades of Grey is released in cinemas around the world.

Spring 2015

Jamie begins filming *The Siege of Jadotville*.